TABLE OF CONTENTS

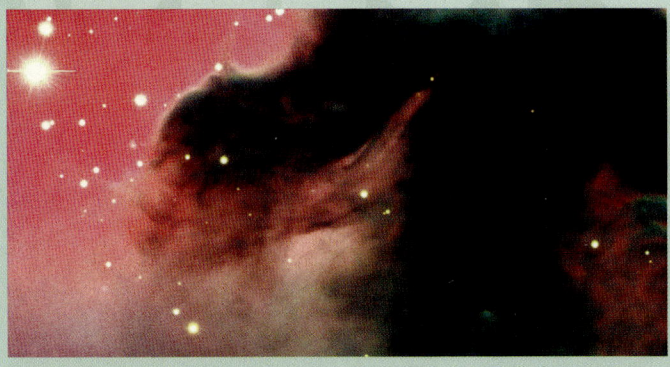

BACK TO THE BEGINNING
SCIENTIFIC DISCOVERIES REVIVE THE ANCIENT BELIEF IN A BEGINNING TO THE UNIVERSE
PAGE 6

WHAT ARE THE ODDS?
IT'S BECOMING CLEAR THAT LIFE ON EARTH IS UNIQUE, AND THE ODDS AGAINST IT EXISTING ELSEWHERE ARE ASTRONOMICAL
PAGE 16

OPTIONS FOR ORIGINS
THE CHOICES IN ACCOUNTING FOR OUR UNIVERSE BOIL DOWN TO THREE — CHANCE, MULTIPLE UNIVERSES, OR DESIGN
PAGE 26

THE PROBLEM WITH HALF AN EYE
CAN INTRICATELY COMPLEX ORGANS LIKE THE EYE BE THE RESULT OF TIME PLUS CHANCE?
PAGE 36

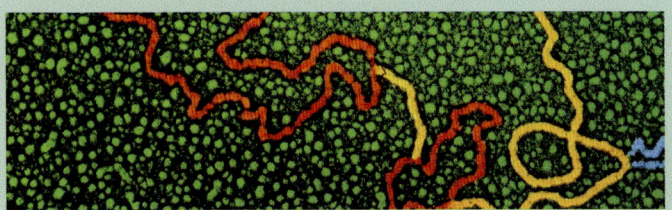

THE LANGUAGE OF OUR CELLS
DOES THE INTELLIGENCE OF DNA POINT TO A DESIGNER?
PAGE 46

THE CASE OF THE MISSING LINKS
WHERE ARE DARWIN'S PREDICTED FOSSILS?
PAGE 64

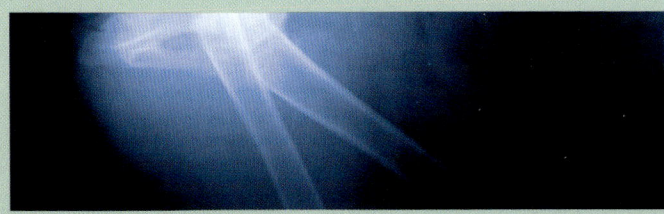

THE HUMAN ENIGMA
EVOLUTIONISTS ARE UNABLE TO EXPLAIN THE ORIGIN OF HUMAN INTELLIGENCE AND CONSCIOUSNESS
PAGE 74

IMAGINE THE DESIGNER
DOES THE UNIVERSE REVEAL CLUES ABOUT THE NATURE OF ITS DESIGNER?
PAGE 84

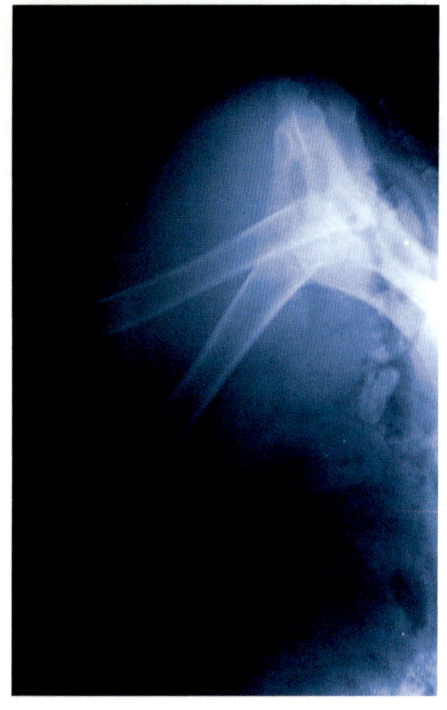 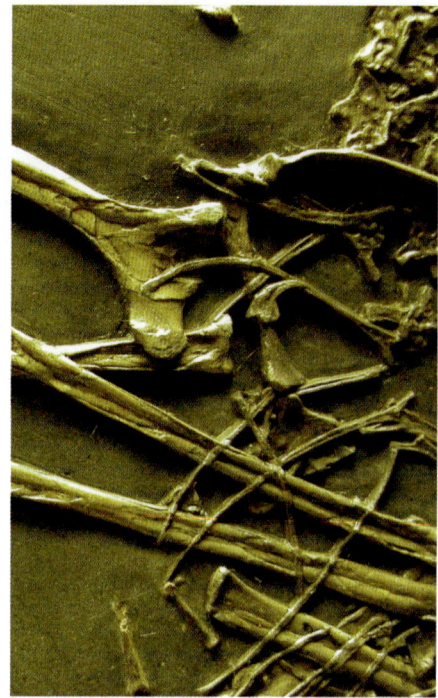 

FROM THE EDITOR

A sunny mountain slope full of skiers and snowboarders exhilarated by the new powder. The first cry of a newborn baby in a maternity ward after hours of labor. A young couple walking along a sunny Hawaiian beach. These are the things that make up what we would call "life." Did it all just happen, or is there some kind of plan or design?

In an interview on CBS's *60 Minutes,* paleontologist Stephen Jay Gould said, "Human beings arose as a kind of glorious accident, surely a kind of glorious cosmic accident." If Gould is right, the universe is random and life is an accident: we just happened to win the cosmic lottery.

Everyone at some point wrestles with the question raised by Gould's interview. Are we here by virtue of a cosmic accident? (And more personally, am I?) Or is there design and purpose woven into the fabric of life? This magazine is devoted to this issue and this question because new discoveries in astronomy, molecular biology, and other scientific disciplines seem to demand a reappraisal. These discoveries have intensified the debate over the origin and purpose of the cosmos.

That debate went public when astronomer and noted author Carl Sagan told a worldwide television audience in the 1980s, "The cosmos is all that is or ever was or ever will be." His convincing manner and visionary language brought a sense of optimism, but when scrutinized, paradoxically, it nullified any sense of personal purpose to life. Sagan's perspective has many labels but is most commonly referred to as "naturalism" or "materialism," which promotes the belief that life in all its complexity is the result of unguided natural processes.

Today, however, a new understanding of our cosmos and the world of microbiology is threatening the paradigm of Darwinian materialism. And this mounting threat is being led by scientists rather than theologians.

The scientists challenging the old paradigm are not some band of religious creationists but rather are women and men willing to ask the difficult questions about materialism, to express doubt about what has turned into faith (naturalistic evolution), and to follow the new trail of evidence though it seems to be leading to a very different conclusion about the origin and nature of our universe.

That conclusion has been expressed in different ways by different scientists, but its common theme is that this universe is not an accident. This dramatic turnaround in scientific thinking, as well as the maelstrom it has created, is evidenced by the August 15th, 2005 Time magazine front cover, entitled, "Evolution Wars."

In one of history's most influential books, The Structure of Scientific Revolutions, Harvard historian and physics instructor Thomas Kuhn observes that old paradigms don't die easily; it takes time and solid evidence to overcome entrenched opposition from the establishment. The evidence convincing a growing cadre of scientists is both solid and compelling.

There is, of course, a less abstract implication of this debate: if the universe is not an accident, then you and I are not accidents either. Such a discovery leads to deep questions like these: How did I get here? What is my purpose? Where do I go after I die? Surprisingly, many scientists have been asking these very questions in light of new discoveries about the cosmos.

You need not be a scientist to hear what leading scientists have concluded about the cosmos. We have done our best within this issue to translate the ideas, concepts, and data to a popular level of understanding. We want to provide a framework for you to be able to make your own evaluations of these new discoveries and see which option makes the most sense to you: an accidental universe or intelligent design.

In that spirit, one of the world's foremost intellects and atheists, Antony Flew, recently arrived at the conclusion that there is an intelligent designer. After 50 years of debating and lecturing against a creator, the new evidence for intelligent design compelled Flew to renounce his atheism. Flew stated his reason, "My whole life has been guided by the principle of Plato's Socrates: Follow the evidence, wherever it leads." We hope you will do the same, or as Morpheus says in The Matrix, see "how deep the rabbit hole goes."

LARRY CHAPMAN

SCIENTIFIC DISCOVERIES REVIVE THE ANCIENT BELIEF IN A BEGINNING TO THE UNIVERSE

IF WE COULD REWIND THE HISTORY OF THE UNIVERSE, WHAT WOULD WE DISCOVER ABOUT ITS ORIGIN AND DEVELOPMENT? DID IT REALLY HAVE A BEGINNING, OR WAS IT ALWAYS THERE?

The influential ancient philosopher Aristotle stated, "It is impossible that movement should ever come into being or cease to be, for it must always have existed. Nor can time come into being or cease to be."

Meanwhile, the biblical book of Genesis famously starts off, "In the beginning God created the heavens and the earth."

Which is it? Is the universe eternal—has it always been here? Or did it have a beginning at some point in time—did it have a birthday, so to speak? These are the two schools of thought that have enrolled followers since early times. (Actually, there was also a third school that postulated that the universe existed on the back of a giant sea turtle, but they're mostly gone now.)

The seesaw of opinion has tipped one way or the other over time. But lately the weight of evidence has all been coming down on the side of the birthday universe.

In the old days when the Christian church dominated Western society, the creation of the universe was taken for granted. But slowly the scientific viewpoint pushed aside creation as well as the creator. Now many scientists are thinking that the idea of a creation may not have been so far off from the truth as they thought. It's looking like the universe had a beginning after all.

Remarkably, one of the first scientists to swing the pendulum of opinion back to the birthday-universe position was so entrenched in eternal-universe thinking that at first he refused to believe his own conclusions.

A GREAT BRAIN'S BIGGEST BLUNDER

When Albert Einstein developed his revolutionary theory of general relativity in 1916, his mathematical calculations pointed to an extraordinary conclusion—the universe was expanding. And since if you rewind the tape on any expansion, you get back to a point where it started, that meant the universe must have had a beginning too.[1]

Einstein, however, was like most scientists of his day in that he believed in an eternal universe. Unwilling to accept a beginning to the universe, Einstein fudged the numbers in order to nullify the conclusion that the universe was expanding.

University of California astrophysicist George Smoot explains that Einstein's main problem with an expanding universe was its implication of a beginning. A beginning pointed to a beginner beyond scientific investigation.[2] However, once experimental data proved that the universe really was expanding, Einstein admitted his error, calling it "the biggest blunder of my life."[3]

There's a point worth considering here: if it could happen to Einstein, it could happen to anyone. Rarely is anyone completely objective when it comes to the issue of a creator. While it is true that religious belief and philosophy became an obstacle for scientific inquiry in the days of Galileo, trends have changed. In the modern era it has been a prejudice against the possibility of a cosmic designer that has kept many scientists from honest and open inquiry.

Thankfully, the truth generally comes out in the end, and scientists began to see the light. For Einstein and others, it was something called red shift that started the parade of evidence for a universe with a beginning.

RED SHIFTING THE BIG BANG THEORY INTO HIGH GEAR

In the late 1920s, the American astronomer Edwin Hubble noticed something unusual as he gazed into the heavens. It wasn't a new planet or little green men waving at him from Mars; it was something more tedious and at the same time more thrilling.

Hubble had been spending countless nights at the Mount Wilson Observatory, studying the stars and galaxies and especially the spectrum of color in the light they sent our way. He discovered that the light from most other galaxies was shifted to the red end of the spectrum, which indicated they were moving away from us. Furthermore, the farther a galaxy was away from us, the more red shifted its light was and, thus, the faster it was moving away from us.

The only explanation for all of this was that space itself was expanding, causing all galaxies to move away from each other. In an expanding universe, from any point in space (including our own), it would appear that most stars and galaxies were racing away. And the farther away they were, the faster they would be racing.

There it was in the red shift: proof that Einstein had been right in the first place (before he fudged his formula) and that the universe really was expanding. Proof, in other words, that the universe was not eternal but had a beginning.[4]

And yet not everyone accepted the proof at first, including a scientist named Sir Fred Hoyle (former Plumian professor of astronomy at Cambridge University and founder of the Institute of Astronomy at Cambridge). Ironically, it was Hoyle who originally described the event as a "big bang," meaning to mock the idea. The name stuck. (According to physics professor Brian Greene, the term "big bang" is actually misleading since there was nothing to explode and no space in which an explosion could take place.)[5] But unlike Hoyle, many other scientists began coming over to the side of the newly named theory.

The world's leading astrophysicist, Stephen Hawking, who has held the esteemed position of Lucasian Professor of Mathematics at Cambridge, calls Hubble's discovery of an expanding universe "one of the great intellectual revolutions of the twentieth century."[6] The discovery that the universe had a beginning has led to a new science called cosmology, which attempts to understand what happened at the origin of the universe, how it works, and what will happen in its future.

The new science led cosmologists to take another look at a seemingly mundane insight from the 19th century, the second law of thermodynamics.

A SECOND LAW OF FIRST IMPORTANCE

In addition to Hubble's discovery, the second law of thermodynamics also predicts a beginning to the universe. You say you don't know the second law of thermodynamics? Think again.

Let's say you come into a room containing me and a bunch of your other pals, and you find a steaming cup of Starbucks coffee on

the table. Being the thoughtful individual that you are, you ask, "Does this belong to anyone?"

To which I reply, "It's been there for the last month."

Well, you'd know immediately I was wrong or lying (probably lying). Why? Because the coffee wouldn't still be hot if it had been there for a month; it would be room temperature.

That's the second law of thermodynamics in action. This law states that everything continually moves from a state of order to disorder and that heat and energy dissipate over time. This is a law that has been verified by proof after scientific proof and has never been shown to be wrong.

Now let's apply this law to the universe, just as cosmologists have. If the universe were eternal, it would have gone cold and lifeless long ago. The stars would have burned out. Planets would have broken up into clouds of dust. And even the black holes would have ceased vacuuming the universe of unsightly stars and planets.

When you see flaming suns and scorching meteors, in other words, you're looking at a steaming cup of coffee that over infinite time would have long since gone room temperature. Since the universe is still full of pockets of heat and energy, it cannot be eternal.

Who would have thought heat would be such a helpful clue? And that's just the half of it.

THE SIGNIFICANCE OF TV INTERFERENCE

There is still another way that the measurement of heat help to prove that the universe is expanding. In the spring of 1964, two researchers at Bell Labs observed a persistent hiss while testing their microwave radiation detector. Regardless of which direction they pointed the antenna, the static was the same. (This is the same static as TV interference. The same static that was supposed to be gone when I paid $150 to have my satellite dish installed.) Those men, Arno Penzias and Robert Wilson, had discovered what scientists say is the echo from the birth of the universe.[7]

But how could scientists know for sure that the hiss they were hearing was actually an echo from the beginning of the universe? Mathematicians calculated that heat generated at the moment the universe began would have been enormous beyond comprehension. This heat would have gradually dissipated over the life of the cosmos, leaving only a tiny residual of about 3 degrees Kelvin (–270 degrees C).

Additionally, in order for galaxies to have formed, the pattern formed by the explosion needed to have slight variations in the form of waves or ripples.

According to George Smoot, these ripples would result in very slight fluctuations in the predicted temperature and would reveal an identifiable pattern.[8] Thus, if the temperatures matched up, the birth of the universe would be scientifically verified. Merely discovering the temperature to be 3 degrees Kelvin would not prove that the universe actually had a beginning; the fluctuations also needed to match.[9]

But how could we verify fluctuations so subtle?

THE GREATEST DISCOVERY OF ALL TIME?

In 1992, a team of astrophysicists led by Smoot launched the COBE satellite in order to verify the temperatures in space. The satellite would be able to take precise measurements and determine whether fluctuations in temperature existed.

The results stunned the scientific world. Not only was the three-degree temperature confirmed, but more importantly, the profiles of the fluctuations were discovered to be a match with what had been expected.[10] Hawking called the discovery "the scientific discovery of the century, if not all time." Smoot himself excitedly stated to news-

paper reporters, "What we have found is evidence for the birth of the universe."[11] He also said, "If you're religious, it's like looking at God."[12]

than ever before.[16] Background radiation measurements exceed 99.9% of what had been predicted.[17] There are now more than 30 independent confirmations that the universe had a one-time origin.[18]

to materialists). Smoot admits, "There is no doubt that a parallel exists between the big bang as an event and the Christian notion of creation from nothing."[22]

THE EVIDENCE HAD BEGUN TO ADD UP, AND SOME SCIENTISTS WEREN'T LIKING THE SUM.

Astounded by the news, Ted Koppel began his ABC *Nightline* television program with an astronomer quoting the opening of Genesis: "In the beginning God created the heavens and the earth." The other special guest, a physicist, immediately added his quote of the third Bible verse: "And God said, 'Let there be light,' and there was light".[13]

Evidence like that provided by the COBE satellite raises some intriguing questions, to say the least.

THE QUESTIONS THAT FOLLOW THE EVIDENCE

Einstein's theorems based on his theory of relativity predict that the universe could not have begun without an outside force or Beginner.[14] Since Einstein's theory of relativity ranks as the most exhaustively tested and best proven principle in physics, his conclusion is deemed correct.[15]

Tests from an array of radio telescopes at the South Pole have confirmed the big bang to a still higher degree of accuracy

New telescopes such as the infrared Spitzer Space Telescope, launched in 2003, have opened up even bigger windows to our universe. They have prompted astronomer Giovanni Fazio, from the Harvard-Smithsonian Center for Astrophysics, to remark, "We are now able for the first time to lift the cosmic veil that has blocked our view."[19]

As a result of the accumulating evidence, the scientific community has long since begun asking questions about origins, such as the following:

- What was there before the big bang?
- Why did the big bang result in a universe enabling life to exist?
- How could everything originate from nothing?

Smoot ponders what was there before the beginning: "Go back further still, beyond the moment of creation—what then? What was there before the big bang? What was there before time began?"[20]

The same astrophysicist notes that "until the late 1910s ... those who didn't take Genesis literally had no reason to believe there had been a beginning."[21] The Genesis account of creation and the big bang theory both speak of everything coming from nothing. Suddenly the Bible and science agree (a discovery somewhat embarrassing

The evidence had begun to add up, and some scientists weren't liking the sum.

TRYING TO AVOID THE BAD DREAM

A beginning to the universe was like a bad dream come true for materialists who wanted to believe everything had always existed. It brought scientists face to face with the logical conclusion that a primary cause must exist. That argument is a simple logical syllogism:

1. Everything that has a beginning had a cause.
2. The universe had a beginning.
3. Therefore, the universe had a cause.

But admitting a cause leads to the next logical question: who or what is the cause?

Think about it for a minute. Since time, space, matter, and motion are all a part of the created universe, then before the beginning it was timeless, spaceless, and motionless.

What can happen spontaneously from this

BACK TO THE BEGINNING • ARTICLE ONE

state of affairs? There's nothing moving, there's nothing colliding, there's … well, nothing. Not even the potential for anything to happen.

The fact that everything came from nothing has forced scientists to acknowledge that something outside of space and time, something very powerful and with apparent volition, must have acted to bring about the beginning. That is, there must have been an intelligent designer of the universe. Some might go ahead and use the name God for this creator.

Well, in certain academic circles, this line of reasoning simply won't do. Thus it is that many materialists have looked for a way to prove that the universe didn't have a beginning. Smoot remarks, "Cosmologists have long struggled to avoid this bad dream by seeking explanations of the universe that avoid the necessity of a beginning."[23]

Sir Fred Hoyle (he who mockingly coined the term "big bang") was one scientist who strongly opposed the concept of a beginning for the universe. In 1948 Hermann Bondi and Thomas Gold joined Hoyle in postulating that matter was in a continual state of creation. They called their idea the steady state theory, which was an attempt to show that the universe is eternal after all, even though the evidence had long been trending against such a view. However, the COBE discovery of background radiation was the fatal blow to the steady state theory.[24]

Next came the oscillating-universe theory. According to this concept, the universe explodes, contracts, and explodes again,

eternally yo-yoing. This would be another way to permit a belief in the eternal existence of the universe. But the physics for this theory didn't work.

More recently, some scientists, including Hawking, have begun considering the so-called multiverse theory. This theory accepts that our universe is finite, but it suggests that ours is just one of many universes. The whole multi-universe may be eternal, according to this theory, even though our particular universe is not. This theory is covered in more depth in another article in this magazine, but the key point to understand about it right now is that it has no evidence whatsoever to support it.

These theories fit neatly with the philosophy of materialism, whereas a beginning of the universe would raise the obvious question, who was there to start it? Professor Dennis Sciama, Hawking's supervisor while he was at Cambridge, admits his reasons for supporting the steady state theory: "I was a supporter of the steady state theory, not in the sense that I believed that it had to be true, but in that I found it so attractive I wanted it to be true."[25]

An origin of the universe meant materialists were suddenly faced with the questions that threatened their worldview.

A ONE TIME BEGINNING

Hoyle and other scientists fervently pursued alternative explanations to a one-time origin of the universe. Eventually, however, the evidence showed clearly that the universe had a beginning, and the big bang theory was proclaimed victorious. Ironically, it was evidence from Hoyle's own research that helped confirm that the universe had a one-time beginning.

Today most cosmologists and physicists accept the big bang theory as the scientific explanation of how our universe began. In fact, scientists believe they can trace the history of the universe all the way back to 10^{-43} of a second. Prior to that point in the history of our universe, all of our current theories break down and science can see no further back. The very beginning of the universe remains a mystery.

Imagine rewinding the universe back to its beginning, a time when there were no stars. No light, matter, or energy. Not even space or time. Suddenly an enormous explosion erupted from this nothingness at a temperature exceeding a million trillion trillion degrees.[26] Time begins along with matter, energy, and space.

When a bomb ejects shrapnel into the air, both the bomb material and the space it blows into have already been there. However, in the beginning of the universe, neither space nor matter existed until the explosion. The space surface of the universe and the newly created matter came into existence.

According to the big bang theory, this explosion launched the entire universe, from the most distant galaxy, to the most colorful nebula, to quasars flashing like beacons, to our own comforting sun and nearby planets, to you and me with our questions about where we came from and what it all means. Since man alone thinks about the meaning and purpose of life, the beginning—and the cause of that beginning—must be fascinating to each one of us.

The verdict is in on whether the universe is eternal or had a beginning. The idea that everything in the cosmos originated out of nothing seems mythical, yet it is now mainstream science.

NOTES

1. Brian Greene, *The Elegant Universe* (New York: Vintage, 2000), 81-82.
2. George Smoot and Keay Davidson, *Wrinkles in Time* (New York: Avon, 1993), 36.
3. Greene, 81-82.
4. Stephen Hawking, *A Brief History of Time* (New York: Bantam, 1990), 38-51.
5. Greene, 83.
6. Hawking, 39.
7. Smoot, 80-83.
8. Ibid., 187.
9. Ibid., 240.
10. Ibid., 241.
11. Associated Press, "U.S. Scientists Find a 'Holy Grail': Ripples at the Edge of the Universe," *International Herald Tribune* (London), April 24, 1992, 1.
12. Thomas H. Maugh II, "Relics of 'Big Bang' Seen for First Time," *Los Angeles Times*, April 1992, A1, A30.
13. *Nightline with Ted Koppel*, ABC, April 25, 1992.
14. Hugh Ross, *The Creator and the Cosmos*, 3rd ed. (Colorado Springs, CO: NavPress, 2001), 224.
15. Roger Penrose, *Shadows of the Mind* (New York: Oxford University Press, 1994), 230.
16. E. M. Leitch et al., "Measurement of Polarization with the Degree Angular Scale Interferometer," *Nature* 420 (2002): 772-87; J. M. Kovac et al., "Detection of Polarization in the Cosmic Microwave Background Using DASI," *Nature* 420 (2002): 772-87; Matias Zalarriaga, "Background Comes to the Fore," *Nature* 420 (2002): 747-48.
17. Gregg Easterbrook, "Before the Big Bang," *U.S. News & World Report* special edition, 2003, 16.
18. Hugh Ross, "Big Bang Passes Test," *Connections*, Qtr 2, 2003.
19. Paul Recer, "Newest Space Telescope: The Spitzer," *Seattle Post Intelligencer*, December 19, 2003, A17.
20. Smoot, 291.
21. Ibid., 30.
22. Ibid., 17.
23. Ibid., 291.
24. Ibid., 86.
25. Stephen Hawking, ed., *Stephen Hawking's A Brief History of Time: A Reader's Companion* (New York: Bantam, 1992), 63.
26. Bradford A. Smith, "New Eyes on the Universe," *National Geographic*, January 1994, 33.
27. Michio Kaku & Jennifer Thompson, *Beyond Einstein*, (New York: Anchor Books, 1995), 167.

IS THE DESIGNER AN ABSENTEE PARENT?

The big bang theory has reopened scientists' minds to the possibility that the universe was created by an intelligent designer. But if so, has that designer remained involved with the universe? Two discoveries, quantum mechanics and string theory, suggest the answer could be yes.

In 1925, Werner Heisenberg shocked the scientific community by showing that the subatomic world is unpredictable. In fact, it behaves unlike anything scientists had ever imagined and seems to betray common sense. This marked the start of the branch of physics known as quantum mechanics, which is the study of the behavior of microscopic particles. (A "quantum," in physicspeak, is the smallest amount of any quantity, such as particles like electrons, quarks, and photons.)

What has fascinated scientists is that particles such as electrons, quarks, and photons can appear from nowhere and disappear just as quickly. No one knows why.

Furthermore, a quantum has an undetermined position until it is observed. When observed, it immediately becomes a particle with a fixed position. Why does this happen? Again, scientists don't have a clue.

In another bizarre phenomenon known as quantum tunneling, a particle can move through a barrier without altering the barrier's structure. Theoretically, the same might be possible for an object or person. Thus, phenomena such as walking untouched through walls—previously thought to be a violation of the laws of physics—are possible.

Physicists have been perplexed at the seeming contradiction of quantum mechanics and relativity, yet they are convinced that there must be some unifying principle. A newer concept in theoretical physics, known as string theory, may solve the riddle of how these bedrock theories are able to coexist in the cosmos.

String theory likens the behavior of particles to tiny vibrating strings. Different vibrations create different behaviors for particles just as different vibrations on a violin or piano string can alter pitch. Among other things, string theory tells us that at the big bang at least six additional dimensions were created along with the four we observe (length, height, width, and time). These additional dimensions are beyond our ability to see or measure.

The implications of string theory on our perception of reality are mind-boggling and require thinking differently about the universe and what is possible. If we could access other dimensions, the following "impossibilities" would be possible.[27]

1. Walking through objects, such as walls
2. Performing surgery without cutting the skin
3. Instant teleportation from one location to another

If these other dimensions exist, a designer could theoretically intervene in our world without being seen. Quantum mechanics and the possibility of other dimensions contradicts materialists' belief that "if we can't see and measure it—it must not exist." But scientists are also baffled about another mystery of the universe that is possibly an even great challenge to materialism: dark matter and energy.

About 95% of the universe is made up of this "dark stuff" that consists of mysterious exotic matter and energy. Although dark matter is invisible, scientists can convincingly measure its gravitational pull. Theoretically, dark matter pervades our very breath. We are on a hurtling spaceship surrounded by an ocean of matter we cannot see!

Two-thirds of the dark stuff consists of "dark energy." Although dark matter is an enigma, dark energy is even more mysterious—scientists have no idea what it is. Some scientists believe dark energy holds the key to understanding the great mysteries of our universe.

This mysterious dark stuff that pervades 95% of the universe, along with the quantum world and other dimensions, have fueled new ideas about how a designer could be actively involved in his universe, yet remain unseen. Is it possible a designer operates in another dimension that intersects ours, or controls hidden quantum particle behavior that undergirds our macro world? Or could he be impacting our world from within the dark 95% of the universe that surrounds us?

Taken together, these mysteries of our universe undermine the materialistic world view, and compel us to face the possibility that our universe was not only *made* but could also be *sustained* and *cared for* by a parent who guides the unseen world with his invisible hand. In that case, the designer could be less like a mother who abandons her newborn and more like a mom who stays with and raises her child.

WHAT ARE THE ODDS?

LIFE IN OUR UNIVERSE IS SO IMPROBABLE THAT IT DEFIES A NATURAL EXPLANATION.

IN HIS MOVIE *SIGNS*, M. NIGHT SHYAMALAN PRESENTS US WITH A PRIEST (PLAYED BY MEL GIBSON) WHO HAS LOST HIS FAITH. THROUGH THE DEATH OF HIS WIFE, THE PRIEST HAS COME TO THE CONCLUSION THAT LIFE IS RANDOM. HE HAS DECIDED THAT HE WILL NO LONGER PRETEND TO SEE GOD IN THE PICTURE.

As Shyamalan zooms in his lens, he shows us that life is without focus: there is no recognizable pattern. But typical of Shyamalan, he turns the lens one more screw to the right, and at this magnification a pattern emerges. Gibson's character is able to see the hand of a great designer lurking behind all that had seemed random. His wife's dying words, his daughter's obsession with water, his son's asthma—everything served a larger purpose.

At the end Mel Gibson returns to the priesthood and makes a blockbuster called *The Passion of the Christ*. Well, not exactly, but his character comes full circle—from faith to skepticism and back to faith. Meanwhile, Shyamalan takes his audience on the same circuitous journey, exploring issues of design and higher purpose in the world.

In many ways the evidence for intelligent design of the universe has come full circle. When early humans looked at the heavens, they could not escape the concept of a creator. In fact, until the 1500s, most people believed in the ancient astronomer Ptolemy's teaching, that Earth was the center of the universe.

But, in the 16th century, Copernicus showed that Earth revolved around the Sun. Suddenly our planet seemed less special. Some astronomers looked out at the universe through telescopes and deduced a creator was unnecessary. Their argument for a materialist worldview was energized by the belief in an ordinary Earth.

Although the founders of modern astronomy strongly believed that the universe was the work of a cosmic genius, these later followers saw the cosmos as totally autonomous and independent of a designer. Copernicus, a strong believer in God, couldn't have disagreed more with such an assumption, and would have taken exception to it.

In the 19th century, this belief in an ordinary Earth became popularized as the "Copernican Principle." This principle has become the bedrock for a materialistic view of the world. However, in the latter part of the 20th century evidence began pouring in about the remarkable fitness of Earth for life.

Scientists have learned that only an exceptionally fine-tuned planet like Earth has the necessary ingredients to harbor life. Additionally, our solar system and galaxy, as well as our entire universe, appear designed to support intelligent life.

The odds that such fine-tuning could have occurred by chance is not just unlikely–scientists say it is virtually impossible.

THEY DON'T CALL THESE NUMBERS ASTRONOMICAL FOR NOTHING

An article in *U.S. News & World Report* remarks, "So far no theory is even close to explaining why physical laws exist, much less why they take the form they do. Standard big bang theory, for example, essentially explains the propitious universe in this way: 'Well, we got lucky.' "[1]

On Christmas Day in 2002, Jack Whitaker, of Scott Depot, West Virginia, got lucky, becoming the largest single-ticket lottery jackpot winner until that time in North America. His prize? A Powerball jackpot of $314.9 million. Over a hundred million other tickets didn't match. What are the odds of that? (And what are the odds that within two years he would be robbed twice, face charges for attacking a bar manager, be sued for making trouble at a nightclub and a racetrack, and be arrested twice for drunk driving? Not nearly as unlikely as his Powerball winning ticket, but still true.)

If someone won even two such lotteries consecutively, we would all assume the results were rigged. And yet, when it comes to life existing in our universe, the odds are far more remote than winning a hundred Powerball lotteries consecutively.

Physicist Paul Davies comments, "The conclusion must be that we live in a world of astronomical unlikelihood."[2]

Donald Page of Princeton's Institute for Advanced Study has calculated that the odds against our universe randomly taking a form suitable for life is one out of 10^{124}, a number beyond imagination.[3]

To try and visualize the difficulty, imagine all the grains of sand on all the beaches on Earth. Then encrypt one grain with a special code known only to you, and randomly bury that grain on a beach somewhere on Earth. (Maybe enjoy a vacation in Maui while you're at it).

The chance a blindfolded person would ever discover that one grain of sand on their first pick is one out of 10^{20} (one chance in 100 billion billion.)

Now offer a reward to anyone who can find it on one pick, even though they don't know which beach to scour, or how deep it is buried. But what if they did? Would anyone believe they discovered it by accident? Yet, scientists tell us that the likelihood of a big bang explosion resulting in a universe able to support life like ours is many times more improbable.

As we consider the odds for the fine-tuning of our universe, galaxy, solar system, and planet, let's keep in mind just how extreme these odds really are. Not just one, but all of them require unbelievably precise fine-tuning. Can such precision be a result of anything other than design? Let's take a look at why many scientists are asking this question.

A FINELY TUNED UNIVERSE

Dr. Robin Collins states in *The Case for a Creator*, "Over the past thirty years or so, scientists have discovered that just about everything about the basic structure of the universe is balanced on a razor's edge."[4] Over 35 different characteristics of the universe and its physical laws must be precisely fine-tuned for physical life to be possible.[5] Following are six of those characteristics:

→ 1. *A large enough expansion rate*. The birth of the universe had to begin with enough force, or life couldn't exist. Stephen Hawking states, "If the rate of expansion one second after the big bang had been smaller by even one part in a hundred thousand million million, the universe would have recollapsed before it ever reached its present size."[6]

→ 2. *A controlled expansion rate*. Although the expansion rate had to be great enough for the universe to avoid a big crunch, if its outward force had been even a fraction greater, that would have been too much for gravity to form stars and planets. Life could never have been possible.[7]

→ 3. *Force of gravity*. If the gravitational force were altered by 0.0000000000000000000000000000000000000001 percent, neither Earth nor our Sun would exist—and you would not be here reading this.[8]

→ 4. *The balance of matter and antimatter*. In the formation of the universe, the balance between matter and antimatter, and the excess of matter over antimatter, needed to be accurate to one part in ten billion for the universe to arise.

→ 5. *The mass density of the universe*. For physical life to exist, the mass density of the universe must be fine-tuned to better than one part in a trillion trillion trillion trillion trillion (10^{60}).[9] Thus, the mass contained in all dark and visible matter, including stars, is essential for the existence of our universe.

"SO FAR NO THEORY IS EVEN CLOSE TO EXPLAINING WHY PHYSICAL LAWS EXIST, MUCH LESS WHY THEY TAKE THE FORM THEY DO. STANDARD BIG BANG THEORY, FOR EXAMPLE, ESSENTIALLY EXPLAINS THE PROPITIOUS UNIVERSE IN THIS WAY: 'WELL, WE GOT LUCKY.'" —U.S. NEWS & WORLD REPORT

- 6. *Space-energy density*. The space-energy density of the universe requires much greater precision than the mass density. For physical life to be possible, it must be fine-tuned to one part in 10^{120}.[10]

According to the big bang theory, all of this minute fine-tuning was programmed into the initial conditions of the first microsecond of the explosion that began our universe. At that instant the rate and ratios of expansion, mass, density, antimatter, matter, etc., were set in place, eventually leading to a habitable planet called Earth.

In addition to the 35 different characteristics of our universe that must be just right for life to exist, our galaxy, solar system, and planet also needed to be exceptionally fine-tuned or we would not be here.[11]

A FINELY TUNED GALAXY

Galaxies are formations of from millions to perhaps a trillion stars. Our own galaxy is called the Milky Way. It's unknown how many galaxies the universe contains, but it may be around a trillion. Surprisingly, given the great number of these star groups, most galaxies are incompatible with life.

In order for life to exist in a galaxy, it needs to meet several criteria.[12] The following are just three of the fine-tuned characteristics a galaxy needs to support life:

- *Shape of the galaxy*. The Milky Way is spiral-shaped. Of the three types of galaxies—elliptical, irregular, and spiral—the spiral type is most capable of hosting human life.

- *Not too large a galaxy*. Our Milky Way is enormous, measuring 100,000 light-years from end to end. However, if it were just a bit larger, too much radiation and too many gravitational disturbances would prohibit life like ours.

- *Not too small a galaxy*. On the other hand, a stable Earth orbit that is necessary for life could not exist if our galaxy were slightly smaller. And a smaller galaxy would result in inadequate heavy elements, such as iron and carbon, essential to life.

Our Milky Way galaxy meets these and many other conditions essential for life. Most of the others do not.

When we focus in even closer, on our own star and its planets, the odds for life being possible become even more extreme.

A FINELY TUNED SOLAR SYSTEM

Copernicus's theory that Earth revolved around the Sun, seemed to relegate our planet to an ordinary status in the universe. However, if Earth was the center of our solar system, as Ptolemy and 16th century Catholic Church leaders had taught, we wouldn't be here. None of them, including Copernicus, knew that in order for human life to be possible, Earth needs to revolve around a Sun that has just the right size, location, and conditions as ours does.

But that is not all. We need other planets such as Jupiter and Mars to act as defense shields, protecting us from a potential catastrophic bombardment of comets and meteors. We also need a moon of just the right size and position to impact our tides and seasons. Let's take a look at just a few of the many conditions in our solar system that are just right for life.

- *The Sun's distance from the center of the galaxy*. Our Sun is positioned thousands of light-years from the center of the Milky Way, near one of its spiral arms.[13] This is the safest part of the galaxy, away from its highly radioactive center.

- *The Sun's mass not too large*. If the mass of the Sun were a small percentage greater, it would burn too quickly and erratically to support life.

- *The Sun's mass not too small*. On the other hand, if it were smaller, its greater flaring would disrupt Earth's rotation rate.

- *The Sun's metal content*. Only two percent of all stars have enough metal content to form planets. Too much metal in a star will allow too many planets to form, creating chaos. Our Sun has just the right amount of metal for planets to form safely.

- *Effect of the Moon*. The Moon stabilizes the Earth's tilt and is responsible for our seasons. If it weren't there, our tilt could swing widely over a large range, making our winters a hundred degrees colder and our summers a hundred degrees warmer.

When astronomers consider our remarkable solar system, they acknowledge that if it was slightly different, advanced biological life would be impossible. But it is not enough to have the right universe, galaxy, and solar system for human life to be possible. The conditions of our home planet must also be fine-tuned to a razor's edge.

A FINELY TUNED PLANET

You may believe that aliens have sent life to Earth from a far distant galaxy (the premise of that memorable drama from 2004, *AVP: Alien vs. Predator*). You may believe that the government is hiding something outer spatial in Nevada's mysterious Area 51. Or you may simply believe that there is undoubtedly intelligent life on other planets. In any case, we have all been raised on the assumption that, given enough time, intelligent life will spring up anywhere in the cosmos (with perhaps a few more eyeballs or reptilian features). Yet new evidence from cosmology is really saying the opposite.

The reality is that we live on an extremely rare planet perfectly positioned in an extremely rare solar system, ideally located in an extremely rare galaxy, within a highly improbable universe. Let's look at our rare Earth.

- → *Water*. Earth has an abundance of water, which is essential for life. Mars once had water and therefore might have harbored life. But water is only one of many requirements for life.

- → *Oxygen*. Earth is the only planet in our solar system in which we can breathe. Attempting to breathe on other planets, such as Mars or Venus, would be instantly fatal, Mars having virtually no atmosphere and Venus having mostly carbon dioxide and almost no oxygen.

- → *Earth's distance from the Sun*. If the Earth were merely one percent closer to the Sun, the oceans would vaporize, preventing the existence of life. On the other hand, if our planet were just two percent farther from the Sun, the oceans would freeze and the rain that enables life would be nonexistent.

- → *Plate tectonic activity on Earth*. Scientists have determined that if the plate tectonic activity were greater, human life could not be sustained and greenhouse-gas reduction would overcompensate for increasing solar luminosity. Yet, if the activity was smaller, life-essential nutrients would not be recycled adequately and greenhouse-gas reduc-

THE MATH MIRACLE

Implicit in all of the scientific discoveries of fine-tuning in the universe is the foundational importance of mathematics to exploring the nature of the universe. Because mathematics is the lens by which we study the universe, we can miss the genius behind the lens itself.

Physicist Eugene Wigner, in a widely quoted paper entitled "The Unreasonable Effectiveness of Mathematics in the Physical Sciences," notes that scientists often take for granted that the math they use to study and quantify the miracles of the universe is miraculous itself. Wigner states, "The enormous usefulness of mathematics is something bordering on the mysterious. … There is no rational explanation for it. … The miracle of the appropriateness of the language of mathematics for the formulation of the laws of physics is a wonderful gift which we neither understand nor deserve."[14]

Such is the nature of mathematics that no one would claim to have invented an equation but only to have discovered or uncovered something that was always true. As the great scientist Johannes Kepler stated, "The chief aim of all investigations of the external world should be to discover the rational order and harmony which has been imposed on it by God and which He revealed to us in the language of mathematics."

Even as we calculate the extreme precision by which the universe was designed, we are alerted to yet another contour of design in the universe: the mathematical laws of

tion would not compensate for increasing solar luminosity.

- *Ozone level in the atmosphere.* Life on Earth survives because the ozone level is within the safe range for habitation. However, if the ozone level were either much less or much greater, plant growth would be inadequate for human life to exist.

For life to exist, these, as well as many other conditions needs to be just right.[15]

ONE BLOOMING ROCK

University of Washington professors Peter Ward and Donald Brownlee conclude in their book, *Rare Earth*, that the conditions favorable for life must be so rare in the universe that "not only intelligent life, but even the simplest of animal life is exceedingly rare in our galaxy and in the universe."[16] This has led their readers to the conclusion expressed by the reviewer from the *New York Times*: "Maybe we are alone in the universe, after all."[17]

If Ward and Brownlee are right, what does that mean to us?

Michael Denton, senior research fellow in human molecular genetics at the University of Otago in New Zealand, tells us why this remarkable fine-tuning has reopened the discussion on the importance of man in our lonely universe.[18]

No other theory or concept imagined by man can equal in boldness and audacity this great claim ... that all the starry heavens, and every species of life, that every characteristic of reality exists for mankind. ... And today, four centuries after the scientific revolution, the doctrine is again reemerging. In the last decades of the twentieth century, its credibility is being enhanced by discoveries in several branches of fundamental science.

It seems ludicrous to claim that life exists on only one tiny speck in a universe of ten billion trillion stars. Yet, incredibly, Earth appears to sit alone in a hostile universe devoid of life, a reality portrayed recently in *National Geographic*:

> If life sprang up through natural processes on the Earth, then the same thing could presumably happen on other worlds. And yet when we look at outer space, we do not see an environment teeming with life.
>
> We see planets and moons where no life as we know it could possibly survive. In fact we see all sorts of wildly different planets and moons—hot places, murky places, ice worlds, gas worlds—and it seems that there are far more ways to be a dead world than a live one.[18]

The incredibly precise numerical values required for life confront scientists with obvious implications. Stephen Hawking observes, "The remarkable fact is that the values of these numbers seem to have been very finely adjusted to make possible the development of life."[19]

NOTES

1. Gregg Easterbrook, "Before the Big Bang," *U.S. News & World Report*, special edition, 2003, 16.
2. Paul Davies, *Other Worlds* (London: Penguin, 1990), 169.
3. Dietrick E. Thompsen, "The Quantum Universe: A Zero-Point Fluctuation?" *Science News*, August 3, 1985, 73.
4. Quoted in Lee Strobel, *The Case for a Creator* (Grand Rapids, MI: Zondervan, 2004), 131.
5. Hugh Ross, *The Creator and the Cosmos*, 3rd ed. (Colorado Springs, CO: NavPress, 2001), 224.
6. Stephen Hawking, *A Brief History of Time* (New York: Bantam, 1990), 121–122.
7. John D. Barrow and George Silk, *The Left Hand of Creation: The Origin and Evolution of the Expanding Universe* (New York: Basic, 1983), 206.
8. Lawrence M. Krauss, "The End of the Age Problem and the Case for a Cosmological Constant Revisited," *Astrophysical Journal* 501 (1998): 461–466.
9. Ross, 53.
10. Ibid., 187.
11. Ibid., 187–193.
12. Guillermo Gonzalez and Jay W. Richards, *The Privileged Planet* (Washington, DC: Regnery, 2004), 132–138.
13. Ibid., 132–138.
14. Eugene Wigner, "The Unreasonable Effectiveness of Mathematics in the Physical Sciences," *Communications on Pure and Applied Mathematics* 13 (1960), 1-14.
15. Ross. 175-199.
16. Peter D. Ward and Donald Brownlee, *Rare Earth* (New York: Copernicus, 2000).
17. William J. Broad, "Maybe We *Are* Alone in the Universe After All," *New York Times*, (February 8, 2000), 1-4.
18. Michael J. Denton, *Nature's Destiny: How the Laws of Biology Reveal Purpose in the Universe* (New York: The Free Press, 1998), 3-4.
19. Joel Achenbach, "Life Beyond Earth," *National Geographic* (January, 2000, Special Millennium Issue), 45.
20. Hawking, 124.
21. Quoted in Strobel, 165.
22. Ibid.

LEADERSHIP UNIVERSITY

THE MEETING PLACE OF FAITH AND REASON. UNIVERSITY PROFESSORS FROM ACROSS THE COUNTRY WRITE FROM THEIR VARIOUS DISCIPLINES ON GOD, SCIENCE, FAITH, AND INTELLIGENT DESIGN.

www.leaderu.com

WATER WORLD

It seems like every other day you see reports in the paper about scientists getting excited that water has been discovered on our Moon. Or on a planet in our solar system. Or on some other celestial body.

From the news stories, you might almost think that all it takes is a little water for life to exist somewhere. Is that true?

In his book *The Case for a Creator*, author Lee Strobel asks Dr. Guillermo Gonzalez, an astrobiologist at Iowa State University, can't one simply find a place in the universe where water stays liquid for a long enough period of time and eventually life may develop?

Gonzalez responds: "It's true that in order to have life you need water—which is the universal solvent—for reactions to take place, as well as carbon, which serves as the core atoms of information carrying structural molecules of life. But you also need a lot more. Humans require twenty-six essential elements; a bacterium about sixteen. The problem is that not just any planetary body will be the source of all those chemical ingredients in the necessary forms and amounts."[21]

Now here is the interesting follow-up question. Strobel asks whether, as science fiction writers have suggested, life couldn't develop in a "radically different form—for instance, creatures based on silicon instead of carbon." In other words, what about all those strange creatures we've seen on *Star Trek*?

Here is Gonzalez's response: "Chemistry is one of the better understood areas of science. We know that you just can't get certain atoms to stick together in sufficient numbers and complexity to give you large molecules like carbon can. You can't get around it. And you just can't get other types of liquids to dissolve as many different kinds of chemicals as you can with water."[22]

The point? Next time you hear about some ice on an asteroid, don't go looking for your distant cousins.

OPTIONS FOR ORIGINS

The choices in accounting for our universe boil down to three: chance, multiple universes, or design

Scientists are looking at the extreme rarity of life in our universe and asking, "why are we so lucky?" At some point you've got to step back from the facts and ask the question "So what does all this fine-tuning add up to?"

Example:

A university student who's just trying to get a passing grade might be satisfied with loading up his short-term memory with the data he's received. But a student who is actually planning to use this information in a career, or for personal enrichment, has to spend some time thinking about the subject's actual meaning.

Same thing with the question of how quasars, Pluto, and you got here.

The evidences for the fine-tuning of the universe to permit life to exist on one medium-sized planet, third from the left, are mounting. Many scientists are speaking in theological terms about what they see as clear evidence for design.

If you were to survey the writings of leading scientists such as Hawking, Penrose, Davies, and Greene, you would find that there are three options being offered for our origins.

- The fine-tuning of the universe is merely a coincidence.
- There are other universes, improving the odds of life.
- The universe has been designed.

LUCKY YOU

Some materialists attribute the fine-tuning of the universe to chance. In *Alpha & Omega*, Charles Seife summarizes how some view the fine-tuning: "It seems like a tremendous coincidence that the universe is suitable for life."[1]

Cosmologists Bernard Carr and Sir Martin Rees state in the journal *Nature*, "Nature does exhibit remarkable coincidences and these do warrant some explanation."[2] In a later article Carr comments, "One would have to conclude either that the features of the universe invoked in support of the Anthropic Principle are only coincidences or that the universe was indeed tailor-made for life. I will leave it to the theologians to ascertain the identity of the tailor."[3]

In other words, *as a scientist, I don't get into religion, so I assume it was all a lucky break*. Scientists who subscribe to a materialistic world view simply can't bring themselves to accept the intervention of an intelligent designer who orchestrated the creation of the universe. Therefore, faced with all the evidence for fine-tuning, they default to the position that it was all just a coincidence.

There is, however, a defense often raised by those who take the viewpoint that life, and the fine-tuning of the universe, are just amazing coincidences. It goes like this: Whatever shape the universe took, one could look at the sequence of events and say that it was just as unlikely that the universe should have developed in that way.

In other words, every state of affairs, from a certain viewpoint, has astronomical odds of its eventuating just the way it did. So why should we really be amazed that we won life's cosmic lottery? Somebody had to.

Let's consider how I lived out my day today as an example of this line of thinking:

What are the odds that I would have gone to the post office, as opposed to the grocery store or Blockbuster, and purchased 18 stamps instead of 20 or 30?

> "THE ODDS AGAINST A UNIVERSE LIKE OURS EMERGING OUT OF SOMETHING LIKE A BIG BANG ARE ENORMOUS... I THINK THERE ARE RELIGIOUS IMPLICATIONS WHENEVER YOU START TO DISCUSS THE ORGINS OF THE UNIVERSE."
>
> STEPHEN HAWKING

What are the odds I would have received a phone call, rather than an e-mail, from my friend Jeff?

What are the odds I would have eaten—today of all days—hot dogs for dinner, when I could have eaten so many other dishes that didn't contain beef hearts?

By the time you get to the end of the day, the odds of my living out my day in exactly this way, as opposed to others, would be rather large. I could get to the end of the day and scratch my head in amazement at the chain of events that have led me to my current sprawled position on my sofa staring at my computer screen—*Gee, what are the odds*?

This is a neat magic trick done with odds, and the inventor of it has a bright career ahead of him as a pollster in politics. Calculating the odds for a particular sequence of ordinary events like my day's circumstances *after* they occur is no different than predicting the winner of a race after it is over. But looking back on a finely-tuned universe and assigning probabilities of it having occurred by chance is totally different. The two scenarios are different as apples and oranges.

In order to calculate the odds against our being here, over a hundred parameters must be balanced on a razor's edge. If just one of them was off by just a slight degree, you wouldn't be reading this.

ADD-ON UNIVERSES

Most scientists don't believe such odds could be a coincidence. So how do materialists explain odds that seem miraculous? If they don't want to acknowledge an intentionally designed universe, they must come up with another scenario that would explain it all, or their materialistic premise is toast. So if you are trying to avoid the implication of a creator, you would want to construct a theory that would decrease the odds of the universe being miraculous.

If you want to avoid the implication of a creator, your tack would be fairly obvious: decrease the odds.

One way you can decrease the odds is to add in the ingredient of several billion years. One might imagine that the universe could plausibly bake up just about anything in that much time, but even the 13.7 billion years that cosmologists estimate for the age of the universe is way too short for life to have reasonably arisen by natural means.

Therefore, some scientists, such as Stephen Hawking and his Cambridge colleague Sir Martin Rees, have taken a different approach. They have speculated that our universe might be merely one of many universes, thus dramatically improving the odds for life in ours. Let's listen to what Rees himself says concerning his motive behind the multi-universe theory:

> If one does not believe in providential design, but still thinks the fine-tuning needs some explanation, there is another perspective—a highly speculative one.... It is the one I prefer, however, even though in our present state of knowledge any such preference can be no more than a hunch....There may be many "universes" of which ours is just one.[4]

Rees and Hawking have persuaded many in the scientific community that other universes are possible, although highly speculative. According to Hawking, the multi-universe theory (also called the multiverse theory) would rule out the need for a designer.[5]

But is the search for other universes driven by science, speculation or a materialistic bias? Seife, a mathematician and journalist for *Science* magazine, explains what he believes to be the motivation behind the multi-universe theory: "Scientists tend to be uncomfortable with coincidences, and the many worlds interpretation gives a way out."[6]

Rees, a materialist, likes the multi-universe theory because it provides an alternative to providential design. The undeniable reality of fine-tuning has energized the multi-universe theory, since it gives hope to the materialist that life could exist without a designer. But many scientists are raising their eyebrows at the speculative nature of the multi-universe theory, considering its premise to be flawed.

IMAGINARY TIME, IMAGINARY UNIVERSES?

Hawking bases his theory on a mathematical concept called imaginary time, which is merely a mathematical concept and doesn't represent reality. By using imaginary time,

Hawking is able to make it appear that the universe never had a beginning. Once again, scientists uncomfortable with a beginning are seeking ways to avoid it. Hawking explains the reason for their avoidance: "So long as the universe had a beginning, we could suppose it had a creator."[7]

Albert Einstein used a different mathematical concept to remove the appearance of a beginning. Later, Einstein admitted it to be his "biggest blunder." According to theoretical physicist Julian Barbour, Hawking's use of imaginary time may also be a blunder. It has been "widely criticized" and has "technical problems."[8]

Most scientists are reluctant to endorse the concept of multiple universes because it isn't based upon any evidence, and can only be theorized in imaginary time. Even its greatest advocates, Hawking and Rees, admit multiple universes can never be empirically verified. In *The Elegant Universe*, Brian Greene calls the multi-universe theory "a huge if."[9]

Physicist Paul Davies explains why materialists are so fervent in their attempts to validate the multi-universe theory.

> Whether it is God, or man, who tosses the dice, turns out to depend on whether multiple universes really exist or not. …
>
> If instead, the other universes are … ghost worlds, we must regard our existence as a miracle of such improbability that it is scarcely credible.[10]

Regarding the multi-universe theory, Davies remarks, "Such a belief must rest on faith rather than observation."[11]

Since the multi-universe theory is based upon faith, most scientists regard it as merely a hypothesis rather than a true scientific theory. Yet it still is being argued as a valid theory by Hawking, Rees, and others who seek a materialistic explanation for our origin. Investigative reporter Gregg Easterbrook, an investigative reporter for the *Atlantic Monthly* concludes his research on

the multi-universe theory by stating: "The multiverse idea rests on assumptions that would be laughed out of town if they came from a religious text."[12]

Hawking and Rees should not be faulted for searching for a workable explanation; that's what scientists do. But this issue raises a red flag, not on Hawking or Rees, but (perhaps) on a fundamental flaw of the scientific method. If it just happened to be true that God really was the cause of something, could science ever discover this truth? Wouldn't science have to offer a materialistic explanation, no matter how unlikely, because the alternative is not an allowable option for them? This is, indeed, a problem, and it's the issue that scientists who do see intelligent design in the cosmos are wrestling with.

HANDMADE UNIVERSE

In *Bringing Down the House*, author Ben Mezrich tells the story of six MIT students applying their skills in logic and mathematics to counting cards and other trickery, who travel to Las Vegas and make millions. they were able to swing the odds in their favor. After a series of winning streaks, they found themselves followed by house detectives who asked them to leave and never return.

How were they discovered? In one sense, they weren't. No one actually ever caught them cheating, but the MIT students did do something that was a dead giveaway: they won. Repeatedly they beat the odds, and when the dealers and house detectives in Las Vegas observe someone repeatedly beating the odds, they suspect intelligent design: someone is not playing by the laws of random chance but by a carefully reasoned system, like card counting.

The fine-tuning in the universe is astounding and unimaginably improbable. It could be all coincidence or chance, or maybe there are multiple universes, raising the odds and probability of life, but a good detective would be wise to consider the distinct possibility that intelligent design lies behind the observable phenomena.

TO HUME IT MAY CONCERN …

It is primarily due to the arguments of 18th-century English philosopher David Hume that science has largely dismissed any argument for design in the universe.

As a materialist, Hume argued that the universe was a result of chance rather than of intentional design. He believed miracles were impossible because they couldn't be subjected to scientific verification.

Hume's arguments refuting intelligent design have been extremely effective in persuading scientists that all events in the world are from chance alone. Hume's basic logic is as follows:

1. The world is ordered.
2. This is due to either chance or design.
3. It is very possible that the world came about by chance.

Hume had several other arguments against design, but according to mathematician William Dembski, he used faulty logic. "Hume incorrectly analyzed the logic of the design argument, for the design argument is, properly speaking, neither an argument from analogy nor an argument from induction but an inference to the best explanation."[13]

Although Hume's influence on science has been pervasive, he lived in a day when astronomy was in its infancy and the prevalent theory favored an eternal universe. He wasn't aware of the big bang theory that points to a beginner, or the design implications of fine-tuning.

The recently discovered fine-tuning of the cosmos has compelled even the most ardent materialists to consider the possibility of intelligent design. What is the best explanation for the fine-tuning? When Hawking first realized that the universe couldn't be a mere coincidence, he related to a reporter, "The odds against a universe like ours emerging out of something like a big bang, are enormous. ... I think clearly there are religious implications whenever you start to discuss the origins of the universe."[14]

Davies concurs. "It seems as though somebody has fine-tuned nature's numbers to make the Universe. ... The impression of design is overwhelming."[15]

Some scientists, such as Hawking, are uncomfortable with the obvious religious implications. But cosmologist Edward Harrison speaks for others who respond to the evidence for the fine-tuning by clearly stating the obvious:

Here is the cosmological proof of the existence of God. ... The fine-tuning of the universe provides prima facie evidence of deistic design.

Take your choice: blind chance that requires multitudes of universes or design that requires only one. ...

Many scientists, when they admit their views, incline toward the ... design argument.[16]

Few scientists believe the precise fine-tuning is merely a coincidence. While some hold to the multi-universe theory, most scientists believe such a speculative theory is beyond the boundaries of science. Many credible scientists have been persuaded by the evidence that our universe is not here by accident but rather is the intentional plan of a superintelligent being.

Dr. Robert Jastrow is a theoretical physicist who joined NASA when it was formed in 1958. Jastrow helped establish the scientific goals for the exploration of the moon during the Apollo lunar landings. He set up and directed NASA's Goddard Institute for Space Studies, which conducts research in astronomy and planetary science. Jastrow wrote these thoughts that summarize the view of many scientists.

For the scientist who has lived by his faith in the power of reason, the story ends like a bad dream.

He has scaled the mountains of ignorance; he is about to conquer the highest peak; as he pulls himself over the final rock, he is greeted by a band of theologians who have been sitting there for centuries.[17]

"THE MULTIVERSE IDEA RESTS ON ASSUMPTIONS THAT WOULD BE LAUGHED OUT OF TOWN IF THEY CAME FROM A RELIGIOUS TEXT."
ATLANTIC MONTHLY

THE ANTHROPIC PRINCIPLE

Astrophysicist Stephen Hawking cites the term "anthropic principle" when attempting to explain why the universe is so exquisitely fine-tuned for life. Hawking writes, "it seems clear that there are relatively few ranges of values for the number that would allow the development of any form of intelligent life. …One can take this either as evidence of a divine purpose in Creation and the choice of the laws of science or as support for the strong anthropic principle."[18] Hawking has advocated the strong anthropic principle solution of many universes in order to avoid the conclusion of a designer.

The anthropic principle is a fancy term for stating the obvious about the fine-tuning of the universe, i.e., if all the conditions in the universe weren't perfect for human life to exist, we wouldn't be here to ask the question of why it is so finely-tuned for life. What sounds like circular reasoning has led to a revival of the argument from design, which had lost its intellectual respectability among many scientists after Darwin.

One aspect of the anthropic principle is that it asserts that our place in the universe is special. This contradicts the general trend of science since Copernicus; that there is nothing special about Earth. (the Copernican principle) Many materialists who dislike the implications, squirm when discussing the anthropic principle, and it remains a controversial topic. But thus far, no scientist has been able to refute the fine-tuning evidence that supports its premise, and many believe it is simply a commonsensical way of saying life on Earth is special.

NOTES

1. Charles Seife, *Alpha and Omega* (New York: Viking Penguin, 2003), 187-188.
2. Hugh Ross, *The Creator and the Cosmos*, 3rd ed. (Colorado Springs, CO: NavPress, 2001), 158.
3. Ibid.
4. Martin Rees, *Our Cosmic Habitat* (London: Phoenix, 2003), 164.
5. Stephen Hawking, *A Brief History of Time* (New York: Bantam, 1990), 127-141.
6. Seife, 222.
7. Hawking, 140-141.
8. Julian Barbour, *The End of Time: The Next Revolution in Physics* (Oxford: Oxford University Press, 1999), 312.
9. Brian Greene, *The Elegant Universe* (New York: Vintage, 2000), 368.
10. Paul Davies, *Other Worlds* (London: Penguin, 1990), 14.
11. Paul Davies, *God and the New Physics* (New York: Simon & Schuster, 1983), 174.
12. Gregg Easterbrook, "The New Convergence," *Wired*, December 2002, Issue 10.12.
13. William A. Dembski, *The Design Revolution* (Downers Grove, IL: InterVarsity Press 2004), 68.
14. John Boslough, *Stephen Hawking's Universe* (New York: Avon, 1989), 109.
15. Paul Davies, *The Cosmic Blueprint* (New York: Simon & Schuster, 1988), 203.
16. Edward Harrison, *Masks of the Universe* (New York: Collier, 1985), 252, 263.
17. Robert Jastrow, *God and the Astronomer* (New York: Norton, 1978), 116.
18. Hawking, 125.

THE LAGOON NEBULA

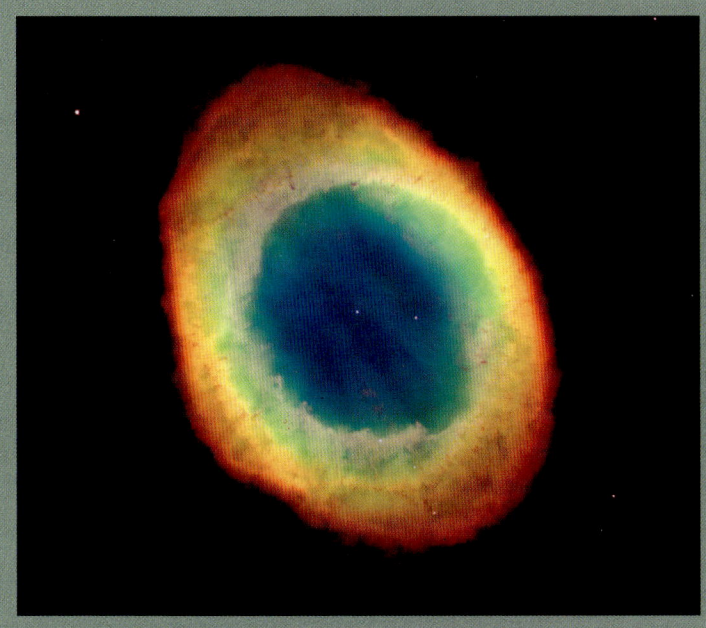

THE RING NEBULA (M57) KNOWN AS "THE EYE OF GOD"

STARS IN THE TARANTULA NEBULA

ULTRAVIOLET LIGHT SOURCE FROM AN ANCIENT GALAXY

THE PROBLEM WITH HALF AN EYE

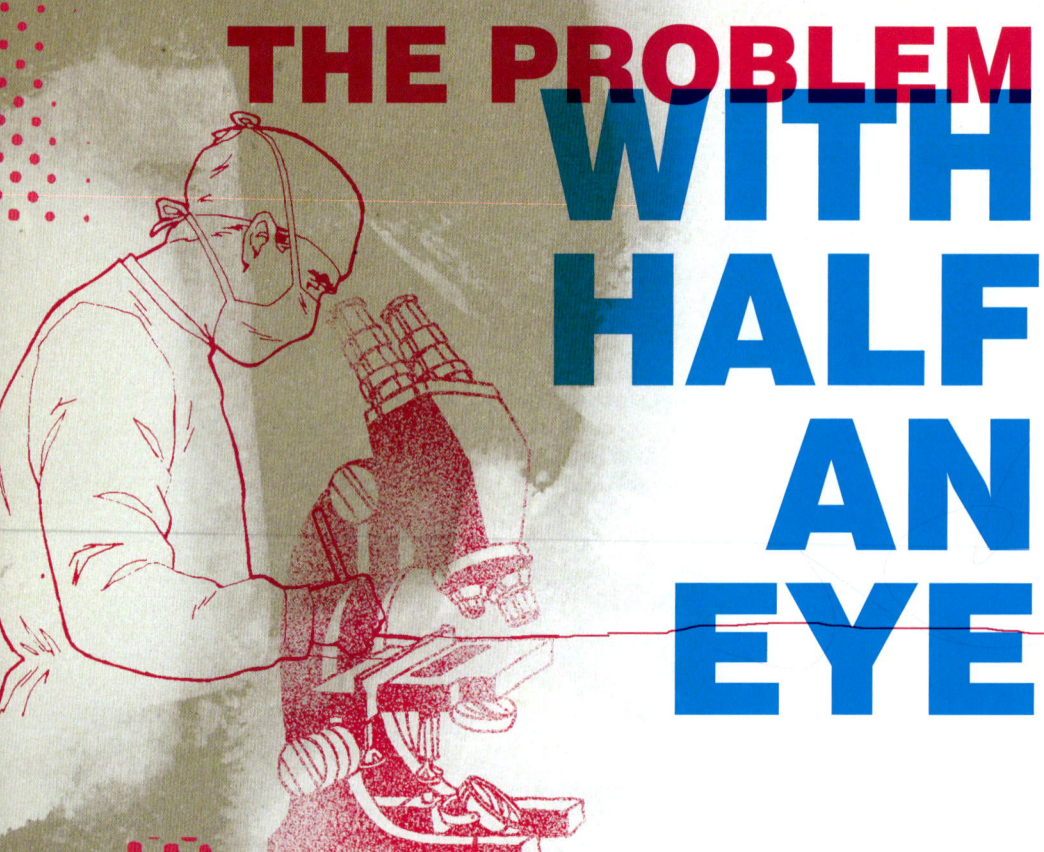

CAN INTRICATELY COMPLEX ORGANS LIKE THE EYE
BE THE RESULT OF TIME PLUS CHANCE?

Looking down at Greenland from 32,000 feet on my trip from Rome to Seattle, I heard a strange noise in the aircraft that sent my blood pressure soaring into hyperspace. Suddenly I began to wonder what would happen if one tiny part on the enormous Boeing 747 failed. Engines, hydraulics, air pressurization—all were complex systems that worked only when several interdependent parts functioned properly.

In vain I sought comfort in my airline pretzels, but comfort can never be found in low-fat foods. I kept thinking of all those dedicated employees (excuse me: "members of the Boeing family") shown on the commercials who apparently love nothing more in life than a well-oiled 747 and who perpetually ponder my safety. But the nagging thought still popped into my head: "Just one faulty or missing part and I'd become part of the first bomb ever to be dropped on Greenland."

In one sense, biological systems are like my Boeing 747: one missing or defective part and they won't work. Here lies one of the major unanswered problems of biology. How did highly complex, interdependent biological systems like the eye develop slowly over eons of time? They would never have worked until fully developed.

Let's step back for a minute and think about all this.

Airplanes, automobiles, cell phones, computers, and other complex machines, can always be traced back to a designer. However, with biological systems, materialists (those who believe nothing exists outside of the material world) assume there is some natural process that created such systems.

The real issue here is whether or not a designer is behind such complexity. There are four possibilities:

1. A designer created biological complexity supernaturally
2. A designer created biological complexity through natural processes
3. A designer combined natural processes and supernatural means to create biological complexity
4. A designer doesn't exist. Complexity came about naturally.

Materialists believe the latter. Scientists who advocate intelligent design generally agree that some superintelligence is behind it all, even though they leave the nature of a designer to theologians.

Here we must look at the evidence to see which of the possibilities makes the most sense. To determine the best option, we need to look closer at complex biological systems to determine whether they can be explained by natural causes alone.

> THE EYE IS LIKE A TELEVISION CAMERA—BUT FAR MORE SOPHISTICATED

THE PROBLEM WITH HALF AN EYE • ARTICLE FOUR • 37

LOOKING AT THE EYE

DARWIN ONCE STATED, "IF IT COULD BE DEMONSTRATED THAT ANY COMPLEX ORGAN EXISTED WHICH COULD NOT POSSIBLY HAVE BEEN FORMED BY NUMEROUS, SUCCESSIVE, SLIGHT MODIFICATIONS, MY THEORY WOULD ABSOLUTELY BREAK DOWN."

The human eye is perhaps the best-known example of a complex system that couldn't just pop up overnight. ("Say, Bill, what's that thing growing on your face?" "I thought it was acne, but now that you mention it, I think I can see out of it.")

With the eye we are not merely dealing with complexity, but with hundreds of separate parts that must work together in unison with incredible precision. Those who study the inner workings of the eye say it operates much like a television camera, but is far more sophisticated. In fact it is more sophisticated than any machine imaginable.

DARWIN'S BIG IDEA

Since the dawn of history, the eye and other complex biological systems had baffled materialists. How could they exist without a designer? However, that changed in 1859 when biologist Charles Darwin published his revolutionary, *The Origin of Species*. The big idea in Darwin's book was that life in all its complexity came about by a process he called *natural selection*. In other words, according to Darwin, no designer is needed. Materialists were elated.

Darwin postulated that natural selection was totally responsible for the complexity of organs like the eye, addressing the issue in a special section entitled, "Organs of Extreme Perfection and Complication."

In his special section Darwin brilliantly argued that the eye might have developed in any number of ways. His reasoning was that even a partially developed eye would offer a creature some evolutionary advantage.

His explanation for the gradual development of such complex systems certainly had its critics, but by and large his ideas were embraced because they helped to explain a great deal of the observable phenomena of our world.

As the evolutionary movement grew, a great deal of evidence seemed to confirm Darwin's theory, evidence similar to what you were taught in your high school textbooks. Adaptability, survival of the fittest, and other Darwinian tenets are clearly demonstrable within a given species. Materialist Richard Dawkins remarks of Darwin's acceptance among most biologists, "Today the theory of evolution is about as much open to doubt as the theory that the earth goes round the sun…."[1]

As an atheist, Dawkins seems to applaud Darwin as the hero behind a purposeless world of chance. He writes, "Darwin's theory of evolution by natural selection is satisfying because it shows us a way in which simplicity could change into complexity, how unordered atoms could group themselves into ever more complex patterns until they ended up manufacturing people. Darwin provides a solution, the only feasible one so far suggested, to the deep problem of our existence."[2]

Since Darwin's theory was birthed in the mid-nineteenth century before the discovery of DNA and the intricacies of how life works at the molecular level, there was no scientific evidence to refute his claims. By the mid-twentieth century, Darwinism had gained widespread acceptance, but mounting evidence persuaded some scientists that his theory was incapable of accounting for life's intricate complexity.

This led to a series of meetings where scientists from various disciplines attempted to hammer out a coherent and unified theory of evolution. The result was called the "evolutionary synthesis," also known as Neo-Darwinism.

But as Dr. Michael Behe, associate professor of biochemistry at Lehigh University, notes in his book *Darwin's Black Box*, "One branch of science was not invited to the meetings [that produced the evolutionary synthesis], and for good reason. It did not yet exist."[3] Behe is referring to his own field of study, biochemistry.

Behe's field did not begin until later in the century, after the advent of the electron microscope. Yet biochemistry is perhaps the most critical of all the disciplines for this study, because it analyzes life at the cellular level and observes the molecular foundations of living organisms.

If Darwin's general theory of evolution is a valid explanation of how life can develop wholly apart from outside intelligence, then it must be demonstrated to be operating at the molecular level. But does Darwin's theory hold up under such scrutiny?

A BETTER MOUSETRAP

Darwin once stated, "If it could be demonstrated that any complex organ existed which could not possibly have been formed by numerous, successive, slight modifications, my theory would absolutely break down."[4] Behe's book, in essence, says, "OK, Charles, take a look at these!" And goes on to cite a handful of examples of what he calls irreducible complexity.

By irreducible complexity, Behe means a single system of interrelated parts, where the absence or failure of any part causes the entire system to non-perform or abort. In the airplane example, it could be a missing wing, rudder, or a defective integral part of the hydraulic system. In the eye, it could be a defective or missing cornea,

retina, pupil, optic nerve, etc. All must work in concert for the eye to see.

So how did each of these separate parts evolve together over eons of time? Could the eye have served any purpose without being complete? We are not merely talking about a half-developed eye, but the eye at all its various stages of development throughout hundreds of millions of years (according to Darwin). Darwin himself stated that his theory (that all life is a product of natural processes alone) stands or falls on its ability to explain how an incomplete organ like the eye can benefit a species.

Behe uses a mousetrap as a nonliving example of irreducible complexity. Five basic parts of the trap must work together in order for it to catch mice: (1) a flat wooden platform; (2) a spring; (3) a sensitive catch that releases when pressure is applied; (4) a metal bar that connects to the catch and holds the hammer back; and (5) the hammer that serves as the instrument of death and cruelty for our harmless mouse.

A mousetrap needs each of these parts to kill mice. Each part works interdependently, and so a partially constructed mousetrap serves no function and is worthless.

Behe's book focuses on a handful of examples, though he states that any biology book contains dozens of them. One of the examples he cites is the microscopic bacterial flagellum, which the bacterium uses as a miniature whiplike rotary motor to propel

itself. The flagellum is a swimming device that works similar to a rotary propeller. It is described by Behe like this:

> Just picture an outboard motor on a boat and you get a pretty good picture of how the flagellum functions, only the flagellum is far more incredible. The flagellum's propeller is long and whiplike, made out of a protein called flagellum. This is attached to a drive shaft by hook protein, which acts as a universal joint, allowing the propeller and drive shaft to rotate freely. Several types of protein act as bushing material (like washer/donut) to allow the drive shaft to penetrate the bacterial wall (like the side of a boat) and attach to a rotary motor. … Not only that, but the propeller can stop spinning within a quarter turn and instantly start spinning the other direction at 10,000 rpms.[5]

> "NOW THAT THE BLACK BOX OF VISION HAS BEEN OPENED, IT IS NO LONGER ENOUGH FOR AN EVOLUTIONARY EXPLANATION...EACH OF THE ANATOMICAL STEPS AND STRUCTURES THAT DARWIN THOUGHT WERE SO SIMPLE ACTUALLY INVOLVED STAGGERINGLY COMPLICATED BIOCHEMICAL PROCESSES THAT CANNOT BE PAPERED OVER WITH RHETORIC."[6]
>
> -Michael Behe
> Professor of Biochemistry

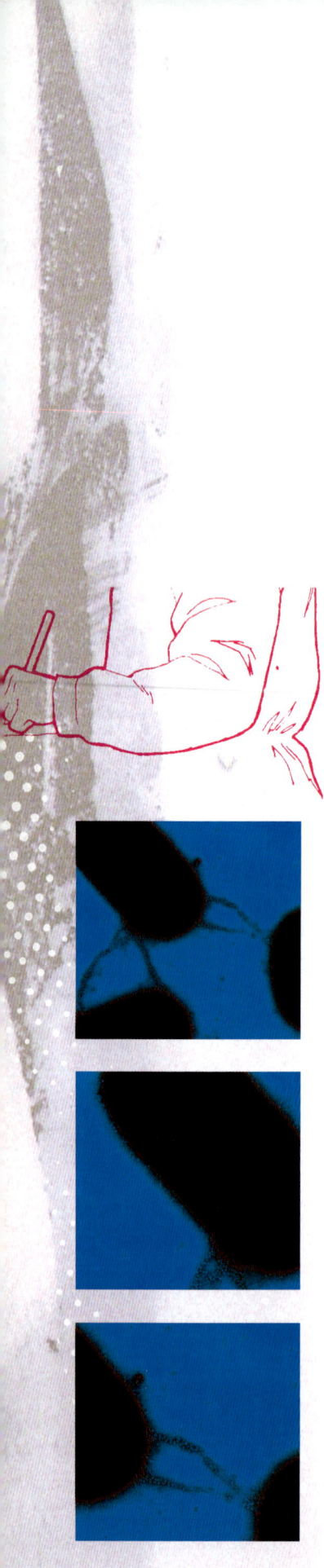

The flagellum's molecular motor requires 20 proteins, all working in synchrony, to function. Like the partially constructed mousetrap, the flagellum would be worthless and perish unless all 20 proteins were fully developed.

Dr. Robert Macnab of Yale University detailed the tiny molecular motor of the E. coli flagellum in a 50 page review, concluding that its development cannot be explained by Darwinian evolution. Labeling Darwin's explanation an "oversimplification," Macnab questions how a non-functional "preflagellum" could have evolved part by part with each being indispensable to its completed function.[7]

Another example Behe cites is what he calls "the intracellular transport system" found within cells. The magnified cell in Darwin's day looked something like an opaque pancake jellyfish with a fuzzy-looking dark spot in the center called the nucleus. It all looked so simple. Only recently, under powerful magnification, have the mysteries of the cell begun to be unveiled.

Molecular biologist Michael Denton uses a similar metaphor to describe the cell's complexity:

> To grasp the reality of life as it has been revealed by molecular biology, we must magnify a cell a thousand million times until it is twenty kilometers in diameter and resembles a giant airship large enough to cover a great city like London or New York. What we would then see would be an object of unparalleled complexity and adaptive design.
>
> On the surface of the cell we would see millions of openings, like the port holes of a vast space ship, opening and closing to allow a continual stream of materials to flow in and out. If we were to enter one of these openings we would find ourselves in a world of supreme technology and bewildering complexity.[8]

But, again, it is not simply complexity; it is irreducible complexity. Going back to Behe's illustration of the mousetrap, everything must be in place for the system to work. Missing just one component, the whole system is worthless. Behe remarks,

> The point of irreducible complexity is…that the trap we're considering right now needs all of its parts to function. The challenge to Darwinian evolution is to get to my trap by means of numerous, successive slight modifications. You can't do it. Besides, you're using your intelligence as you try. Remember, the audacious claim of Darwinian evolution is that it can put together complex systems with no intelligence at all.[9]

FINGERPRINTS OF A DESIGNER?

Several materialists have taken issue with Behe's case for irreducible complexity, but none have adequately explained a process by which such complex organs and systems have evolved by mere chance.

Surprised at the sudden maelstrom caused by his book, Behe defends his position in *The Boston Review*. "The rotary nature of the flagellum has been recognized for about

25 years. During that time not a single paper has been published in the biochemical literature even attempting to show how such a machine might have developed by natural selection."[10]

In *The Flagellum Unspun*, Ken Miller argues against irreducible complexity, labeling Behe and other intelligent design advocates, "unimaginative."

Dr. William Dembski rebuts Miller's objection by stating, "The problem is not that we in the intelligent design community...just can't imagine how those systems arose.... Darwin's theory, without which nothing in biology is supposed to make sense, in fact offers no insight into how the flagellum arose."[11]

EACH HUMAN EYE...
- HAS OVER 100 MILLION RODS
- HANDLES 1.5 MILLION SIMULTANEOUS MESSAGES
- MOVES 100,000 TIMES EACH DAY
- HAS AUTOMATIC FOCUSING
- HAS SIX MILLION CONES
- CAN DISTINGISH AMONG SEVEN MILLION COLORS[13]

James Shapiro, a biochemist at the University of Chicago, concurs, "There are no detailed Darwinian accounts for the evolution of any fundamental biochemical or cellular system, only a variety of wishful speculations."[12]

Darwin's Black Box is a scientific book, not a theological one, but Behe has been joined by a growing number of scientists who claim they see the fingerprints of intelligent design within irreducibly complex biological systems. One of them, cosmologist Allan Sandage has remarked: "The world is too complicated in all its parts and interconnections to be due to chance alone. ... The more one learns of biochemistry the more unbelievable it becomes unless there is some type of organizing principle—an architect for believers."[14]

EXTREME PERFECTION AND COMPLICATION, INDEED

We began this article by mentioning the objection of the human eye as it was raised and addressed by Darwin. For most people coming to grips with the implications of materialistic evolution, complex structures like the human eye are not simply a hard pill to swallow but rather a chicken bone stuck in the throat. Intuitively, we struggle to imagine how such a structure could slowly develop over time and what use a half-developed eye would serve.

A careful reading of Darwin's explanation in "Organs of Extreme Perfection and Complication" reveals that he never answers the problem. In fact, regarding how the eye got started, Darwin stated, "How a nerve comes to be sensitive to light hardly concerns us more than how life itself originated."[15]

Did Darwin really believe the eye evolved bit by bit over time? Although his theory attempts to explain how it could have happened, many believe Darwin himself was unconvinced. Years after he had written his world-changing theory Darwin admitted to a friend, "The eye to this day gives me a cold shudder."[16] Hmm...

> "THE MORE ONE LEARNS OF BIOCHEMISTRY THE MORE UNBELIEVABLE IT BECOMES UNLESS THERE IS SOME TYPE OF ORGANIZING PRINCIPLE— AN ARCHITECT FOR BELIEVERS."
>
> Allan Sandage, Cosmologist

NOTES

1. Richard Dawkins, *The Selfish Gene* (Oxford: Oxford University Press, 1989),1.
2. Ibid.,12.
3. Michael Behe, *Darwin's Black Box* (New York: Free Press, 2003), 24.
4. Charles Darwin, *Origin of Species* (New York: Bantam Books, 1999), 158.
5. Behe, 22.
6. Quoted in Lee Strobel, *The Case for a Creator* (Grand Rapids, MI: Zondervan, 2004), 199.
7. Macnab, R. (1978), "Bacterial Mobility and Chemotaxis: The Molecular Biology of a Behavioral System," *CRC Critical Reviews in Biochemistry*, vol. 5, issue 4, Dec., 291-341.
8. Michael Denton, *Evolution: A Theory in Crisis* (Chevy Chase, MD, Adler & Adler, 1986), 328.
9. Quoted in Lee Strobel, *The Case for a Creator*, 199.
10. Michael Behe, "The Sterility of Darwinism," *Boston Review*, February/March 1997.
11. William Dembski, "Still Spinning Just Fine: A Response to Ken Miller", William Dembski@baylor ed 2.17.03, v.1.01.
12. James Shapiro, "In the details...what?" *National Review*, (September 16, 1996), 62-65.
13. Hugh Davson, *Physiology of the Eye*, 5th ed., (New York: McGraw Hill, 1991).
14. Allan Sandage, "A Scientist Reflects on Religious Belief," *Truth: An Interdisciplinary Journal of Christian Thought*, Vol. 1, (1985).
15. Darwin, 156.
16. Charles Darwin (1860) in letter to Asa Gray, F. Darwin, ed;, *The Life and Letters of Charles Darwin*, vol. 2, (London: John Murray, 1888), 273.

EVERYSTUDENT.COM

A SAFE PLACE TO EXPLORE QUESTIONS ABOUT GOD

DISCOVERY INSTITUTE

Presents the newest and most compelling case for Intelligent Design!

The DVD igniting the debate over Darwinism and Design!

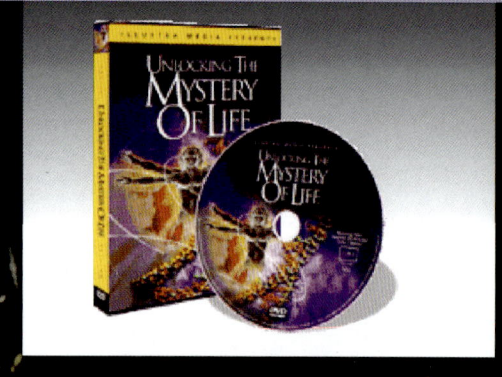

CENTER FOR SCIENCE AND CULTURE

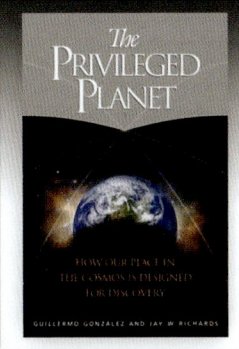

THE LANGUAGE OF OUR CELLS

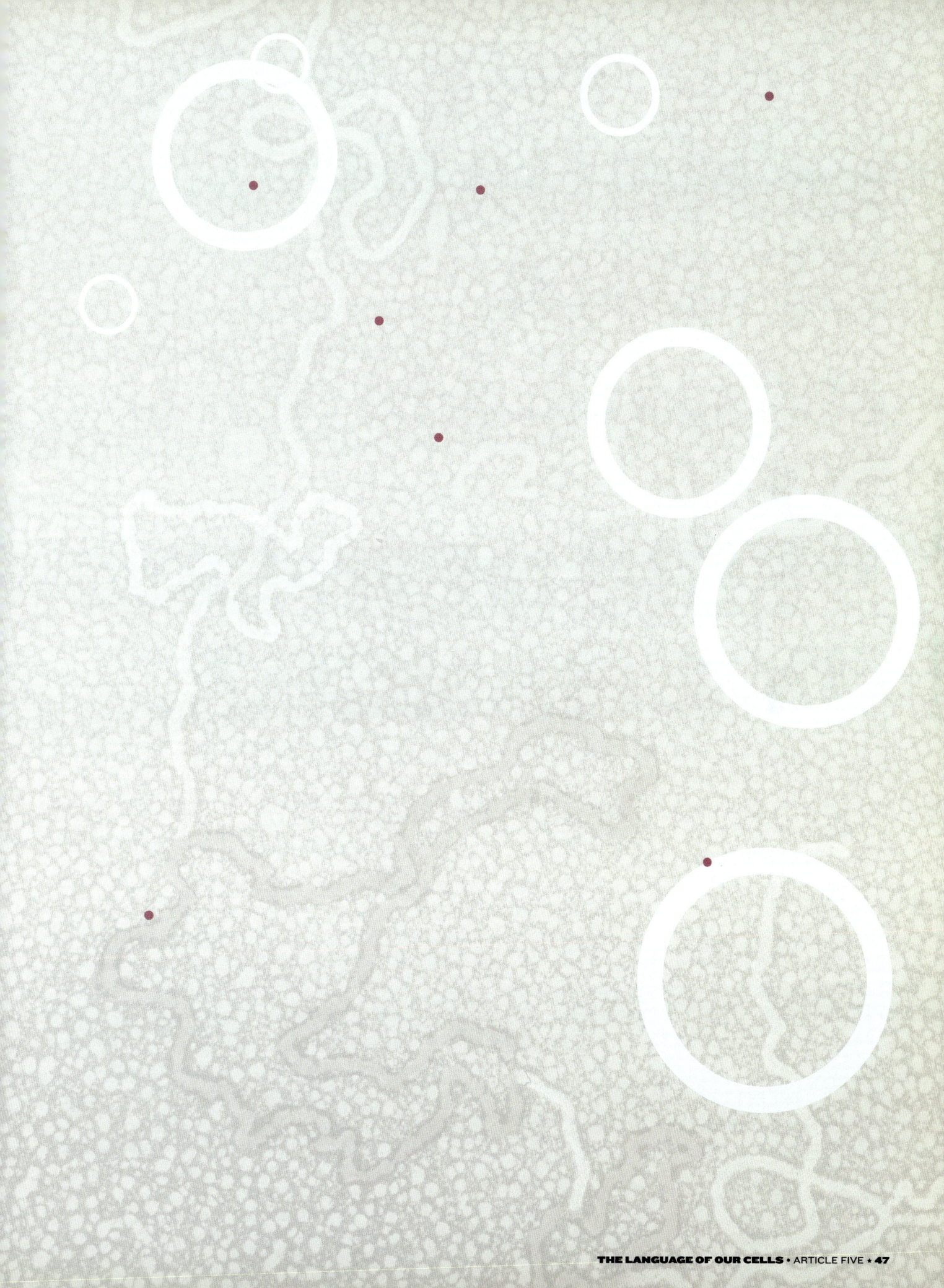

WAS THE LANGUAGE OF DNA PROGRAMMED BY A DESIGNER—OR BY CHANCE?

OF CLOTHES DRYERS, MOUNT RUSHMORE, AND PRIME NUMBERS

Consider for a moment the cathedral-like structure of a snowflake under a microscope. Look at the beauty. Look at the complexity. Look at the originality of each individual flake. Surely this is evidence for a grand designer in the universe.

Well, no, actually it's not—no more so than the burned enchilada of a woman in Mexico that apparently revealed the image of Jesus (though in the photo it did kind of look like him).

Although crystalline forms of a snowflake are beautiful and impressive, designs of this type abound in nature, and natural processes can and do produce them.

Neo-Darwinists believe that natural selection and favorable mutations are the total explanation for the appearance of design in nature.

But what if complexity in nature is discovered that is not explainable by natural selection and chance mutations? What if, unlike our snowflake and enchilada examples, scientists discover a form of complexity that exceeds all human engineering and all sophisticated software programs? This raises an important question: How would we be able to detect intelligent design in nature if it actually exists?

The folks at SETI (Search for Extraterrestrial Intelligence) have done some thinking along the lines of what constitutes signs of intelligence. They are searching for extraterrestrial life, as opposed to God, but they have to deal with the same problem set. How would they recognize communication from outer space if they saw or heard it? Some of their thinking is brought out in the movie *Contact*. In one scene, the character played by Jodie Foster spends the evening listening to her dryer (presumably Blockbuster was closed). But there is a method to her apparent madness. She is trying to train her ears so that she will be able to recognize intelligent radio signals from outer space, filtering out the zillion random signals produced by all manner of objects in the cosmos.

A clothes dryer produces a certain level of mechanical rhythm; its noise actually has a level of design, sort of like that of a snowflake. But that noise (especially when you have sneakers thumping around in there) represents a type of design that nonintelligence (that is, nature) can produce.

How can we tell the difference between design that occurs naturally and intelligent design?

Let's say we've headed out to Vegas, and along the way, we come upon a bizarre rock formation. I say, "Hey, look at the erosion on that rock. It looks kind of like Richard Nixon when the Watergate tapes were made public." You, on the other hand, think it looks like Vladimir Putin eating scrambled eggs. We agree to disagree, but we both note that the forces of erosion made something that looks a bit like a product of intelligent design.

Now, as we drive farther, we come to Mount Rushmore. Seeing it for the first time, I am amazed. I say, "Wow, look at the erosion on those rocks. It looks just like three presidents I recognize and some guy wearing glasses." You rightly call me an idiot, not only because you know who Teddy Roosevelt is, but also because it is obvious by the way the stone is cut and the extraordinary degree of design that this is the product of intelligent craftsmen—ones who apparently have no fear of heights. But there must be a more scientific way to differentiate between these two levels of design: one that can be produced by nature and one that can't.

Later on in the movie *Contact*, the scientists receive radio waves at the sequence of 1,126 beats and pauses. The sequence, they deduce, represents the prime numbers 2 through 101. It becomes doubtful that random radio waves could emit such a sequence, thus they presume they have made contact.

This is a more scientific way of differentiating between two different orders of design. It is commonly called *CSI*. This acronym has nothing to do with a popular TV show. It stands for "complex, specified information."

CSI: THE UNIVERSE

Here is what you need to remember about CSI, or complex, specified information. Nature can generate information that is complex, and it can produce information that is specified, but it cannot do both.

The best way to understand this is to think of yourself as a computer programmer. (You might want to grab a large bag of potato chips and a six-pack of Coke to get into character.) I want you to write a program for the computer telling it to type random letters of the alphabet.

It should be fairly easy to write the program. Just instruct the computer to type keys at random and repeat the process infinitely. Now, occasionally the letters might make an interesting pattern, perhaps even type the word "Nixon" by accident, but it is clearly generating a design of complexity without any real specificity.

Now let's switch it around. Let's say I ask you to program the computer to type the word "the". This is going to require specificity. You must specify, "Computer, type the letter 't,' then 'h,' and then 'e,' and do this over and over again until your printer runs out of ink or your hard drive crashes." This is specific, but it is not complex. You can program the computer in this case, like the previous one, with just a few lines of instructions.

Typing random letters or typing a simple word over and over is like the kind of design that natural processes can handle on their own.

Now let's look at specified complexity. Let's say I ask you to program the computer to write out a Harlequin romance novel and make the girl decide to dump the guy in the end. You would have to write a list of instructions for the computer larger than the book itself. You would have to specify, in the form of a command, every letter of every word.

Few people would have thought of Harlequin romances as specified complexity, but as you can see, they are. The commands to the computer are extremely complex and extremely specific. That's the kind of detail we must demand if we are going to believe that there is intelligent design exhibited in the world.

PROBABLY INTELLIGENT

Seems simple enough, but at what point does something cross the threshold from the simple design found in nature to second-order design produced only by intelligence? Mathematician William Dembski illustrates the difference by having us visualize a rat trying to go through a maze.

In a simple maze, the rat can take one turn and escape from the maze. Even a dim-witted rat could take one turn and escape. But now imagine that the maze is extremely complex, possessing walls and requiring 100 precise turns to reach the point of escape. How likely is it that the little critter will quickly learn all the correct turns and escape? Impossible–unless we have one awfully bright rat.

So, when do we infer intelligence? According to mathematicians when the odds against an event occurring are 1 in 10^{150} or greater, it *can't* be accidential.[1] In order to grasp such an astronomical number, consider that the odds against winning a Power ball lottery with a single ticket is about 1 in 10^8. Or trying to pick a solitary atom from all the atoms in the universe would be 1 in 10^{80}.

So, having cleared all that up, we come to the real question. Forgetting all the erosion and snowflake patterns, are there any examples of specified complexity found in nature pointing toward intelligent design? The short answer is yes. What follows, without getting into too much detail, is the longer answer. It uses the example of something each of us has heard something about: deoxyribonucleic acid, or DNA.

WHAT A LITTLE STRAND CAN DO

DNA. That one complex molecule contains the complete blueprint for every cell in every living thing. In a sense DNA is like a recipe where common ingredients are used to make different dishes. Only, instead of tasty dishes, DNA instructs cells to make flowers, whales, chickens, or people. (Hmm…so chickens aren't tasty dishes?)

The genius of DNA lies not only in its complex coded instructions for life but also in its incredibly well-designed architecture, which allows it to contain billions of detailed instructions within a microscopic molecule. The amount of DNA that would fit on a pinhead contains information equivalent to that of a stack of paperback books that would encircle the earth 5,000 times![2]

Our complete blueprint is present in each of our thousand million million cells. Think of an enormous building with thousands upon thousands of rooms, where each room houses a complete set of blueprints for the entire structure. (If these analogies are getting a little sterile for you, then you might want to imagine a series of beach houses—and imagine yourself sitting in one.) However, instead of merely thousands of rooms, our bodies contain trillions of cells, each with a complete package of DNA instructions.[3]

Each strand of DNA in our bodies consists of three billion base pairs of genetic information. These base pairs form a chain, which constitutes the entire human genetic code. Today the entire human genome has been mapped out. Even though humans are closest to chimpanzees in DNA sequencing, there are still some 40 million differences. (Except maybe with my friend Bob.)[4]

YOUR CELLS ARE TALKING

But just what is DNA, and how does it work? Although scientists are only beginning to unravel its mysteries, they know that DNA works much like a coded language. Microsoft chairman Bill Gates (apparently sizing up the potential to patent it and make it a part of Windows) discloses, "DNA is like a computer program, but far, far more advanced than any software we've ever created."[5]

When we think of sophisticated computer programs, we immediately realize that their coded software was intentionally designed. Materialists believe that DNA originated without any such intentional process. But is it possible that natural causes alone engineered DNA?

Prior to microbiologists' discovery of the incredibly complex language of DNA, materialists had believed its origin was explainable by natural means. However, design theorists have now applied the mathematical discipline of CSI to the question of whether DNA is the result of intelligent design or was accidental in its origin.

Historian and philosopher Stephen C. Meyer comments on the intelligence required for coded languages: "Our experience with information-intensive systems (especially codes and languages) indicates that such systems always come from an intelligent source."[6]

In other words, like a code or language, DNA operates with specifically organized instructions. This is the CSI (complex, specified information) discussed earlier as the watermark of intelligent design.

When DNA directs the cell to make proteins, it first gives instructions to make amino acids. Then twenty different amino acids must precisely link up into a chain, folding into an exacting, irregular three-dimensional protein. The amino acids are like letters; their arrangement spells out the specific protein being made.

Proteins are truly amazing. MIT-trained scientist Dr. Gerald Schroeder explains,

> Other than sex and blood cells, every cell in your body is making approximately two thousand proteins every second. A protein is a combination of three hundred to over a thousand amino acids. An adult human body is made of approximately seventy-five trillion cells. Every second of every minute of every day, your body and every body is organizing on the order of 150 thousand thousand thousand thousand thousand amino acids into carefully constructed chains of proteins. Every second; every minute; every day. The fabric from which we and all life are built is being continually rewoven at a most astoundingly rapid rate.[7]

LIFE IN A TEST TUBE?

In the 1950's, Harold Urey, a professor at the University of Chicago challenged his students to create life in a test tube. One of his students who tried, Stanley Miller was jubilant, when after enormous efforts he produced a few amino acids…the building blocks of proteins.

It all appeared so promising, but what Miller didn't understand then was that without DNA, those amino acids would never be able to form proteins…the stuff of life. The initial euphoria faded once further discoveries revealed life's incredible complexity.

Professor J.P. Moreland compares laboratory results with the complexity required to generate life: "…if life can be likened to an encyclopedia in complexity and information, the best we have done is to synthesize a compound which carries the complexity and information of the word ME. The jump from ME to an encyclopedia is so far and speculative that the relevance of progress so far is questionable."[8]

Meyer points out that the chemical codes directing the process attach themselves to the structure of the DNA molecule like letters on a chalkboard, but they do so without becoming organically involved with the board or the other letters. Therefore, he distinguishes the information content from the chemical bonding.

Furthermore, Meyer compares the sequencing of the amino acids to a language: "Amino acids alone do not make proteins, any more than letters alone make words, sentences or poetry."[9]

The fact that the arrangement of the letters is not the result of chemical bonding has driven Meyer to conclude that, without intelligence, DNA would never be able to turn amino acids into proteins. He writes, "The chance of each amino acid finding the correct bond is one in twenty; the chance of one hundred amino acids hooking up to successfully make a functional protein is one in 10^{30}."[10]

And to survive, the protein chain must be contained within an intricate cellular architecture. That means that the odds against a protein being manufactured randomly are astronomical. It would be easier for a blindfolded person to find one special grain of sand hidden on one of the world's beaches than to have a protein appear by chance.

WHERE DID IT COME FROM?

Such complexity is so improbable that Meyer believes the DNA code cannot be the product of undirected natural processes. Furthermore, he reasons that DNA coding exhibits creative intelligence beyond random chemical bonds.

Perhaps this is why every attempt to create life has failed. Cambridge Professor of Evolutionary Paleobiology, Simon Conway Morris remarks on biologists' efforts to replicate life in a test tube: "And yet, something is clearly missing: life cannot be created in the laboratory, nor is there any clear prospect of it happening."[11]

How did a molecule with such complex coded instructions originate? What natural process triggered a smattering of organic chemicals to come together and form the incredibly sophisticated double helix? Schroeder remarks, "And here's that enigma. … It shows its head in a dozen different ways, the problem of how the entire process originally got started."[12]

Dembski, Meyer, and Schroeder are part of a growing number of scientists and mathematicians who have concluded that the DNA molecule is so complex that it couldn't have spontaneously assembled itself.

In *Probability 1*, mathematician and evolutionist Amir Aczel summarizes the DNA dilemma: "Having surveyed the discovery of the structure of DNA … and having seen how DNA stores and manipulates tremendous amounts of information (3 billion separate bits for a human being) and uses the information to control life, we are left with one big question: What created DNA?"[13]

An increasing number of scientists in other fields are also admitting that DNA's complexity is not explainable by mere chance. Theoretical physicist Paul Davies affirms in *The 5th Miracle*,

> The peculiarity of biological complexity makes genes seem almost like impossible objects. …
>
> I have come to the conclusion that no familiar law of nature could produce such a structure from incoherent chemicals with the inevitability that some scientists assert.[14]

Biologist Michael Behe comments on the dilemma facing scientists who are wedded to a purely materialistic account of the origin of life, "In the face of the enormous complexity that modern biochemistry has uncovered in the cell, the scientific community is paralyzed."[15]

Agnostic Sir Fred Hoyle, when considering the enormous information requirement of life writes, "Were a refined theory available for estimating the information content of DNA it would, in our opinion, be immediately apparent from its overwhelming content that life could never have arisen on a miniscule planet like on Earth. It would be seen that, to match the information content of even the simplest cell, nothing less than the resources of the entire Universe are needed."[16]

DNA BY DESIGN?

Scientists have been stunned by the overwhelming probability against DNA forming by chance. It is one thing for intelligent scientists to manipulate chemicals under laboratory conditions, and it is quite another to attribute the origin of DNA to random action. Even the most ardent materialists do not claim to have explained DNA's origin.

Amir Aczel questions his own materialistic belief by admitting that DNA is too complex to have arisen from natural processes. In a reflective mode he asks,

> Are we witnessing here something so wondrous, so fantastically complex, that it could not be chemistry or random interactions of elements, but something far beyond our understanding?[17]

DNA's codiscoverer Francis Crick also considers DNA to be too complex to have arisen in a warm pond on early Earth. This highly regarded Nobel Prize–winning biologist concludes, "An honest man, armed with all the knowledge available to us now, could only state that in some sense, the origin of life appears at the moment to almost be a miracle, so many are the conditions which would have had to have been satisfied to get it going."[18]

In spite of Crick's assertion that DNA appears miraculous he remained a materialist and began looking to outer space for the origin of life. (panspermia).

Having acknowledged the impossibility of DNA to originate naturally, some scientists have shifted their focus to RNA. Several biologists believe that DNA emerged from RNA. However, microbiologists who have analyzed RNA now believe it too "could not have emerged straight from the prehistoric muck."[19]

Not only is RNA prohibitively intricate, but it's far more delicate than DNA, meaning it couldn't cohere by itself even if it did come together by chance. Thus, the origin of life remains an unsolved riddle to scientists.

Aczel reasons that the complexity of DNA could not have arisen naturally on Earth, He asks, "Was it perhaps the power, thinking, and will of a supreme being that created this self-replicating basis of all life?"[20] Like Crick, Aczel concludes that DNA must have arrived from outer space.

But according to Dembski, "Natural causes such as chance and law are incapable of producing CSI."[21] Since these laws apply throughout the universe, one shouldn't hold his breath about finding Klingons on Planet Qo'noS in the Beta Quadrant—unless a designer made DNA based life elsewhere.

So how did life on Earth originate? Is intelligent design worthy of consideration? Not according to Dawkins, Eldridge, Mayr, and a host of other materialistic scientists who are convinced it is an enemy of science. Yet other leading scientists are willing to objectively look at the evidence. And new scientific evidence has pushed intelligent design to the forefront of the debate on origins. Even many hardened atheists have considered the evidence and admit the implications of design.

Antony Flew is one materialist who led the charge against an intelligent designer. Recognized by many as the world's leading atheist for the past fifty years, Flew wrote over thirty books arguing against a creator.

But this formidable atheist took an honest look at DNA, remarking,

> What I think the DNA material has done is show that intelligence must have been involved in getting these extraordinarily diverse elements together. The enormous complexity by which the results were achieved look to me like the work of intelligence.[22]

Flew, who accepts Darwinian evolution, but doubts it can account for life's origins, sees intelligent design as the best option to explain biological complexity. He made front page news when he renounced his atheism, remarking,

> I think the argument to Intelligent Design is enormously stronger than it was when I first met it...It now seems to me that the finding of more than fifty years of DNA research have provided materials for a new and enormously powerful argument to design.[23]

Flew's honesty is to be applauded, but materialists aren't clapping. As the intelligent design movement gains momentum, many refuse to consider it as an option, dismissing it as "unscientific." However, most thinking people want to hear the facts and draw their own conclusions. Like Flew, many who have honestly investigated the evidence, are in awe at what appears to be a superintelligence behind life and all its intricate complexity.

> "It now seems to me that the finding of more than fifty years of DNA research have provided materials for a new and enormously powerful argument to design."
>
> Antony Flew
> former leading atheist

NOTES

1. William A. Dembski, *The Design Revolution* (Downers Grove, IL: InterVarsity Press, 2004), 85.
2. Werner Gitt, "Dazzling Designs in Miniature," *Creation Ex Nihilo*, December 1997–February 1998, 6.
3. Richard Dawkins, *The Selfish Gene* (Oxford: Oxford University Press, 1989), 1.
4. Nicholas Wade, "In Chimpanzee DNA, Signs of Y Chromosome's Evolution," *New York Times*, Sept. 1, 2005, A13.
5. William A. Dembski and James M. Kushiner, eds., *Signs of Intelligence* (Grand Rapids, MI: Brazos, 2001), 108.
6. Ibid., 115.
7. Gerald Schroeder, *The Hidden Face of God* (New York: Touchstone, 2001), 189.
8. Ibid.
9. J.P. Moreland, *Scaling the Secular City* (Grand rapids: Baker Books, 2000), 221.
10. Larry Witham, *By Design* (San Francisco: Encounter, 2003), 147.
11. Simon Conway Morris, *Life's Solution* (Cambridge: Cambridge University Press, 2003), 46.
12. Schroeder, 192–193.
13. Amir D. Aczel, *Probability 1* (New York: Harvest, 1998), 88.
14. Paul Davies, *The 5th Miracle* (New York: Simon & Schuster, 2000), 20.
15. Michael J. Behe, *Darwin's Black Box* (New York: Touchstone, 1996), 185.
16. Sir Fred Hoyle, "The Information Content of Life," *The Universe Unfolding* (Oxford: Clarendon Press, eds. Sir Hermann Bondi & Miranda Weston-Smith, 1998), 8.
17. Aczel, 88.
18. Francis Crick, *Life Itself* (New York: Simon & Schuster, 1981), 88.
19. Nell Boyce, "Triumph of the Helix," *U. S. News & World Report*, February 24/March 3, 2003, 41.
20. Aczel, 88.
21. William A. Dembski, *Intelligent Design: the Bridge between Science and Theology* (Downers Grove, IL: InterVarsity), 1999.
22. Antony Flew, quoted in video, *"Has Science Discovered God?"* Roy Abraham Varghese's Institute for Metascientific Research in Garland, Texas, December, 2004.
23. Quoted in Gary Habermas, "My Pilgrimage from Atheism to Theism": Interview with Antony Flew, *Philosophia Christi*, (Winter, 2005).

WHAT SETI IS LOOKING FOR

The scientists at SETI (Search for Extraterrestrial Intelligence) are searching for radio signals from outer space that contain complex, specified information (CSI), which would prove the transmissions were not random but the result of intelligent communication. They employ four criteria in examining radio signals.

1. Spikes. These are radio waves occurring at single frequencies that are strong enough to be distinguished from general noise.

2. Gaussians. Radio signals from a distant transmitter should get stronger and then weaker as the telescope's focal point moves across that area of the sky. Specifically, the power should increase and then decrease with a bell-shaped curve (a gaussian curve). Gaussian curve-fitting is an excellent test to determine if a radio wave was generated "out there" rather than being a simple source of interference somewhere here on Earth, since signals originating from Earth will typically show constant power patterns rather than curves.

3. Pulses. Our alien neighbors may not be sending out a nice, even tone for us to detect. They may be sending a series of spaced pulses—a more economical use of power.

4. Triplets. A triplet is a set of three equally spaced spikes. The SETI@home screensaver tests for triplets by looking at every pair of spikes above a certain threshold power. It then looks for another spike precisely between the two spikes. If one is found, a triplet is logged and sent back for further study.

"Are we witnessing here something so wonderous, so fantastically complex, that it could not be chemistry or random interactions of elements, but something far beyond our understanding?"

Professor Amir Aczel

THE RACE TO DISCOVER THE SECRET OF LIFE

Is it possible to know how life operates at a molecular level? Since Darwin, efforts had accelerated to discover the secret of life. Why we are different from each other and from other forms of life? How do the same chemicals form flowers, snakes, and humans?

In 1944, 85 years after Darwin published his theory, a team led by Oswald Avery discovered that a molecule of DNA carries genetic information. But no one knew what it looked like or had any idea of its importance.

That same year physicist Erwin Schrödinger wrote a little book entitled *What Is Life?* Schrödinger speculated that genetic material might be contained in a chemical code within cells' chromosomes, arguing that the storage and transmission of information was an essential component of life. But was it actually possible to discover the mystery of life? Biologists knew that behind all of life there must be some type of elaborate code that instructed cells in what to produce.

The race to discover life's great secret began in earnest in 1951 when physicist Linus Pauling determined the molecular structure of the protein keratin. Although a physicist, Pauling was a leading expert on chemical bonding. After Pauling's discovery, he and others began to focus their attention on DNA, a nucleic acid present within the cell. But what was the molecule like? How could a molecule, too tiny to be observed even by the most powerful electron microscope, contain the complex coding to make a human being?

In October of 1951 biologist James Watson met Francis Crick at the Cavendish Laboratory in Cambridge, England, and the two began collaborating on research into the structure of DNA. They had hoped that discovering its structure would reveal the mystery of how genetic information was stored and transferred to make life.

In November, Watson attended a seminar held by a brilliant research chemist from King's College—Rosalind Franklin, nicknamed Rosy. Franklin was an expert with X-ray crystallography, a technique able to precisely map the location of atoms within a crystal. Using this technique, Franklin was able to determine that DNA had a twisted shape (helix) with at least two strands.

With that discovery, Franklin was perilously close to discovering DNA's structure. In 1952 she accomplished the incredible feat of creating an X-ray image of the molecule, strongly suggesting it was a double or triple helix. Although Franklin was close, more tests would need to be conducted to determine its true architecture.

Pauling was convinced that DNA was a triple helix, not a double helix. Watson and Crick followed suit until Franklin spotted their error and generously put them on the right track. However, in December of 1952, Watson and Crick heard that Pauling was getting ready to publish a paper on the structure of DNA. It appeared they had been beaten. But Pauling had made a basic chemical mistake, depicting the molecule with three strands. This would mean DNA was not an acid, and Watson and Crick knew it must be an acid. After seeing Pauling's paper in January, Watson and Crick jubilantly toasted Pauling's error in the Eagle pub.

A colleague of Franklin's at King's College, Maurice Wilkins, had met Watson earlier at a lecture in Naples, Italy. Wilkins had been working with X-ray diffraction to determine DNA's structure. However, the prickly Franklin and her colleague had a falling out, and Wilkins began surreptitiously confiding information to Watson.

Suddenly, the breakthrough for Watson and Crick came when Watson saw a copy of Franklin's X-ray image shown to them by Wilkins. This gave them the clues they needed to solve the mystery.

OnFebruary 28, 1953, the puzzle pieces came together. Watson and Crick, they had discovered the long-mysterious double-helix architecture of DNA. It was the twisted shape of the molecule that enabled it to pack so much information into such a small area. Four simple chemicals enabled DNA to encode the entire blueprint for a living creature within each cell. So simple, yet so ingenious and so incredibly complex.

At the end of the day Crick walked into the Eagle pub in Cambridge, brashly announcing that he and Watson had "found the secret of life." On April 25 they published their discovery in a letter to the journal *Nature*. Rosalind Franklin was elated at the discovery, even though little credit was given to her at the time. She died of ovarian cancer at the age of 37, before the Nobel Prize was awarded to Watson and Crick.

IN THE POPULAR PRESS

While often confined to back-alley brawls in the scientific journals, occasionally the intelligent design debate bubbles up into more popular periodicals, those with a higher subscription rate than, oh, *The Origin of Biological Information and the Higher Taxonomic Categories* and *Molecular Machines: Experimental Support for the Design Inference*.

Recently, *Wired*'s cover story was entitled "The Plot to Kill Evolution." It's a little slanted, at least for *Wired*, exposing their latent desire to see machinery evolve intelligence, with just a touch of paranoia that intelligent design is a conspiracy as opposed to a theory. But as the theory continues to gain ground, even *Wired* allows for a member of their own fold to make his case for intelligent design—the "technogeek guru of bandwidth," George Gilder. In his sidebar Gilder discusses the complex information processing of DNA and RNA in human beings, stating,

It is a process subject to the mathematical theory of information, which shows that even mutations occurring in cells at the gigahertz pace of a Pentium 4 and selected at the rate of a Google search engine couldn't beget the intricate interwoven fabric of structure and function of a human being in such a short amount of time.

The contrary notion [to intelligent design] that the world bubbled up randomly from a prebiotic brew has inspired all the reductionist futilities of the 20th century [by which he means Marxism, among other things]. ... In biology classes, our students are not learning the largely mathematical facts of the 21st century; they're imbibing the consolations of a faith-driven 19th century materialist myth.

Gilder gets few points for tact, but he does state the case succinctly while the opposition maintains the reliable posture of name-calling: somehow the theory of intelligent design is a "plot" against Darwin and a conspiracy hell-bent on bringing us back to the days of a flat earth and Vatican-controlled laboratories. More and more people are seeing through the ad hominem attacks against intelligent design, realizing they are based on rhetoric rather than evidence.

from the Washington Times
SCIENCE, 'FRAUDS' TRIGGER A DECLINE IN ATHEISM
By Uwe Siemon-Netto

Two developments are plaguing atheism these days. One is that it appears to be losing its scientific underpinnings. The other is the historical experience of hundreds of millions of people worldwide that atheists are in no position to claim the moral high ground.

British philosopher Anthony Flew, once as hard-nosed a humanist as any, has turned his back on atheism, saying it is impossible for evolution to account for the fact that one single cell can carry more data than all the volumes of the Encyclopedia Britannica.

Mr. Flew still does not accept the God of the Bible. But he has embraced the concept of intelligent design — a stunning desertion of a former intellectual ambassador of secular humanism to the belief in some form of intelligence behind the design of the universe.

A few years ago, European scientists snickered when studies in the United States — for example, at Harvard and Duke universities — showed a correlation between faith, prayer and recovery from illness. Now 1,200 studies at research centers around the world have come to similar conclusions, according to "Psychologie Heute," a German journal, citing, for example, the marked improvement of multiple sclerosis patients in Germany's Ruhr District because of "spiritual resources."

Atheism's other Achilles' heels are the acts on inhumanity and lunacy committed in its name. "With time, [atheism] turned out to have just as many frauds, psychopaths and careerists as religion does. ... With Stalin and Madalyn Murray O'Hair, atheism seems to have ended up mimicking the vices of the Spanish Inquisition and the worst televangelists, respectively," Mr. McGrath wrote in Christianity Today.

The Rev. Paul M. Zulehner, dean of Vienna University's divinity school and one of the world's most distinguished sociologists of religion, said atheists in Europe have become "an infinitesimally small group. There are not enough of them to be used for sociological research," he said.

Mr. Zulehner cautioned, however, that the decline of atheism in Europe does not mean that re-Christianization is taking place. "What we are observing instead is a re-paganization," he said.

The Rev. Gerald McDermott, an Episcopal priest and professor of religion and philosophy at Roanoke College in Salem, Va., said a similar phenomenon is taking place in the United States. "The rise of all sorts of paganism is creating a false spirituality that proves to be a more dangerous rival to the Christian faith than atheism," he said. After all, a Satanist is also "spiritual." Mr. Pannenberg, a Lutheran, praised the Roman Catholic Church for handling this peril more wisely than many of his fellow Protestants. "The Catholics stick to the central message of Christianity without making any concessions in the ethical realm," he said, referring to issues such as same-sex "marriages" and abortion.

In a similar vein, Mr. Zulehner, a Catholic, sees Christianity's greatest opportunity when its message addresses two seemingly irreconcilable quests of contemporary humanity — the quest for freedom and truth. "Christianity alone affirms that truth and God's dependability are inseparable properties to which freedom is linked."

As for the "peril of spirituality," Mr. Zulehner sounded quite sanguine. He concluded from his research that in the long run, the survival of worldviews should be expected to follow this lineup: "The great world religions are best placed," he said.

As a distant second he sees the diffuse forms of spirituality. Atheism, he said, will come in at the tail end.

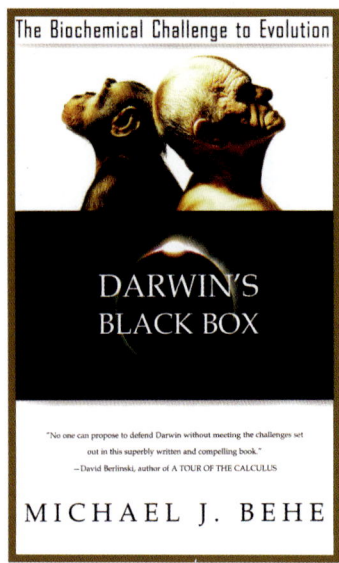

DARWIN'S BLACK BOX
THE BIOCHEMICAL CHALLENGE TO EVOLUTION

MICHAEL J. BEHE
Free Press, 1996, 307 pages, paperback

Michael Behe, associate professor of biochemistry at Lehigh University, argues that the most convincing evidence for intelligent design is not to be found in the stars or the fossils but in biochemical systems. Behe faces two challenges: (1) to demonstrate at the molecular level that gradual mutations could not produce the cell's complexity; and (2) to make the subject readable and understandable to the layman. He does both.

Behe uses examples such as vision, blood clotting, and cellular transport to demonstrate that life comprises an astonishing array of chemical machines, made up of finely calibrated, interdependent parts that could not have developed gradually. These systems, says Behe, are "irreducibly complex." That is, all their parts must exist for the system to function, making their progressive development highly problematic.

The strength of Behe's argument lies in his thorough knowledge of his subject and the examples he cites. You clearly get that this is not the fruit of someone else's footnotes but of his own personal analysis. Meanwhile, Behe well documents the professional science literature on the subject and shows its complete silence on the subject, preferring no explanation for how the complex systems within a cell might have developed by undirected forces.

Here is a book written with the layman in mind.

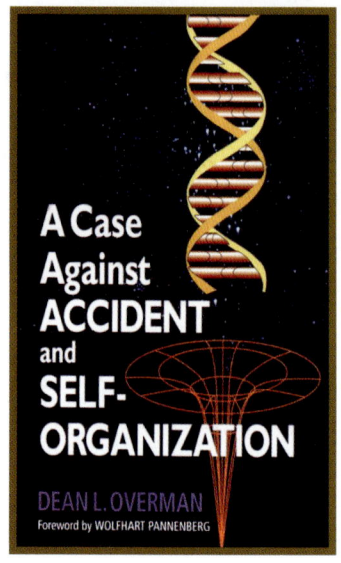

A CASE AGAINST ACCIDENT AND SELF-ORGANIZATION
A MATHEMATICAL ANALYSIS OF LIFE'S PROCESSES

DEAN L. OVERMAN
Paperback edition 2001, Rowman & Littlefield.

This book isn't for laymen or the scientifically challenged. Dean Overman uses logic and mathematical calculations to answer the questions perplexing biologists and astrophysicists—and us. Is it mathematically possible that accidental processes could have caused the formation of living matter from nonliving matter? Could accidental processes have caused the formation of a universe compatible with life? Are current self-organization scenarios for the formation of the first living matter plausible?

Overman answers "no" to these questions and proceeds to demonstrate the mathematical impossibility that accidental processes produced the first living matter.

The author examines other issues related to the creation of the universe, including Stephen Hawking's no-boundary proposal, the need for a Creator as the preserving cause of the universe, and the explanations offered by the weak and strong anthropic principles. The centerpiece of the book, though, is its handling of the topic of self-organization. Unfortunately, Overman avoids some of the details of the theory, and the devil is always in the details. What you get is a primer on the topic, not a thorough analysis.

These days a lot of unexplained design is being swept under the self-organization rug, so this book is a helpful beginning in addressing the subject.

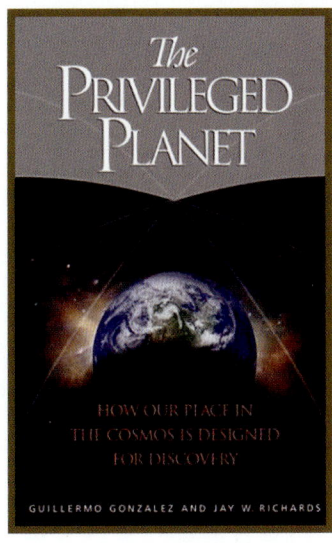

THE PRIVILEGED PLANET
HOW OUR PLACE IN THE COSMOS IS DESIGNED FOR DISCOVERY

**GUILLERMO GONZALEZ
JAY RICHARDS**

2004 (Hardcover edition), Regnery Publishing, Inc., 464 pp.

"The Earth is a very small stage in a vast cosmic arena. … Our posturings, our imagined self-importance, the delusion that we have some privileged position in the Universe, are challenged by this point of pale light." —Carl Sagan, *Pale Blue Dot*, 1994

In *The Privileged Planet* astronomer Guillermo Gonzalez and philosopher Jay W. Richards confront the claim made by Carl Sagan a decade ago, when they argue that Earth, in fact, is unique in the universe—there is nothing else like it. Richards and Gonzalez demonstrate that our planet is exquisitely fit, not only to support life, but also to give us a superb view of the universe, as if Earth—and the universe itself—were designed both for life and for scientific discovery.

According to Gonzalez and Richards, something seems "fishy" about Earth's privileged place in our universe. The authors then conclude, "At some point, this pattern should lead us to not only re-evaluate certain entrenched assumptions about the universe but even to reconsider our very purpose."

The *Privileged Planet* is an exceptionally well written and informative book that asks the tough questions about the remarkable new discoveries in our universe. It is also available in video and DVD formats, and has recently been aired on Public Television.

A MEANINGFUL WORLD
REVEALS A UNIVERSE SHOT THROUGH WITH MEANING, DESIGNED TO BE INTELLIGIBLE ON MULTIPLE LEVELS.

**BENJAMIN WIKER
JONATHAN WITT**

Meaningful or meaningless? Purposeful or pointless? When we look at nature, whether at our living earth or into deepest space, what do we find?

In stark contrast to contemporary claims that the world is meaningless, Benjamin Wiker and Jonathan Witt reveal a cosmos charged with both meaning and purpose. Their journey begins in Shakespeare and ranges through Euclid's geometry, the fine-tuning of the laws of physics, the Periodic Table of Elements, the artistry of ordinary substances like carbon and water, the intricacy of biological organisms, and the irreducible drama of scientific exploration itself. Along the way, Wiker and Witt fashion a robust argument from evidence in nature, one that rests neither on religious presuppositions nor on a simplistic view of nature as the best of all possible worlds. In their exploration of the cosmos, Wiker and Witt find all of the challenges and surprises, all of the mystery and elegance one expects from a work of genius.

"MY RELIGION CONSISTS OF A HUMBLE ADMIRATION OF THE ILLIMITABLE SUPERIOR SPIRIT WHO REVEALS HIMSELF IN THE SLIGHTEST DETAILS WE ARE ABLE TO PERCEIVE WITH OUR FRAIL AND FEEBLE MINDS."

"BEFORE GOD WE ARE ALL EQUALLY WISE – EQUALLY FOOLISH."

"EVERYONE WHO IS SERIOUSLY INVOLVED IN THE PURSUIT OF SCIENCE BECOMES CONVINCED THAT A SPIRIT IS MANIFEST IN THE LAWS OF THE UNIVERSE -- A SPIRIT VASTLY SUPERIOR TO THAT OF MAN."

"THE SCIENTIST IS POSSESSED BY THE SENSE OF UNIVERSAL CAUSATION...HIS RELIGIOUS FEELING TAKES THE FORM OF A

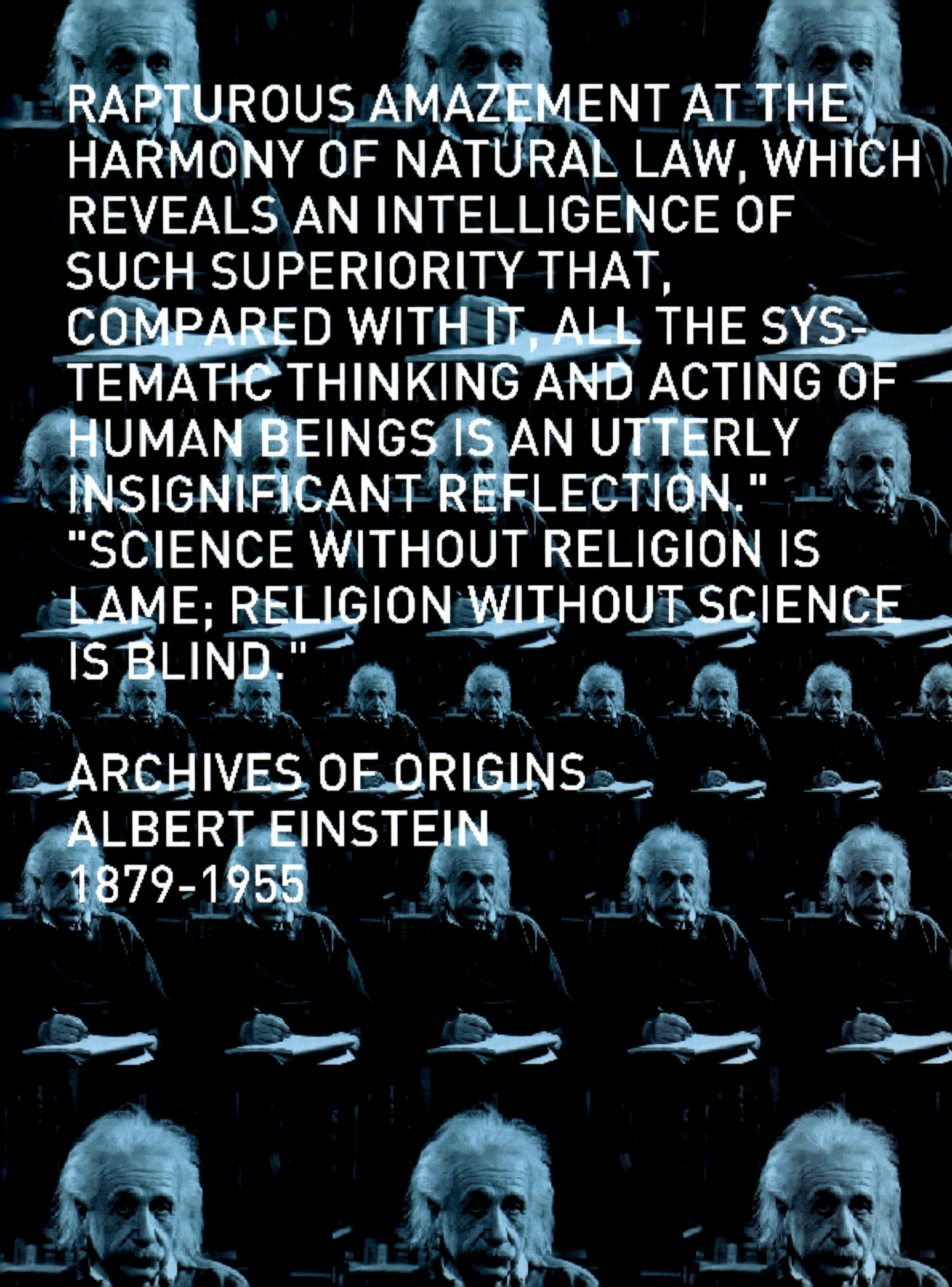

"RAPTUROUS AMAZEMENT AT THE HARMONY OF NATURAL LAW, WHICH REVEALS AN INTELLIGENCE OF SUCH SUPERIORITY THAT, COMPARED WITH IT, ALL THE SYSTEMATIC THINKING AND ACTING OF HUMAN BEINGS IS AN UTTERLY INSIGNIFICANT REFLECTION."

"SCIENCE WITHOUT RELIGION IS LAME; RELIGION WITHOUT SCIENCE IS BLIND."

ARCHIVES OF ORIGINS
ALBERT EINSTEIN
1879-1955

THE CASE OF THE MISSING LINKS

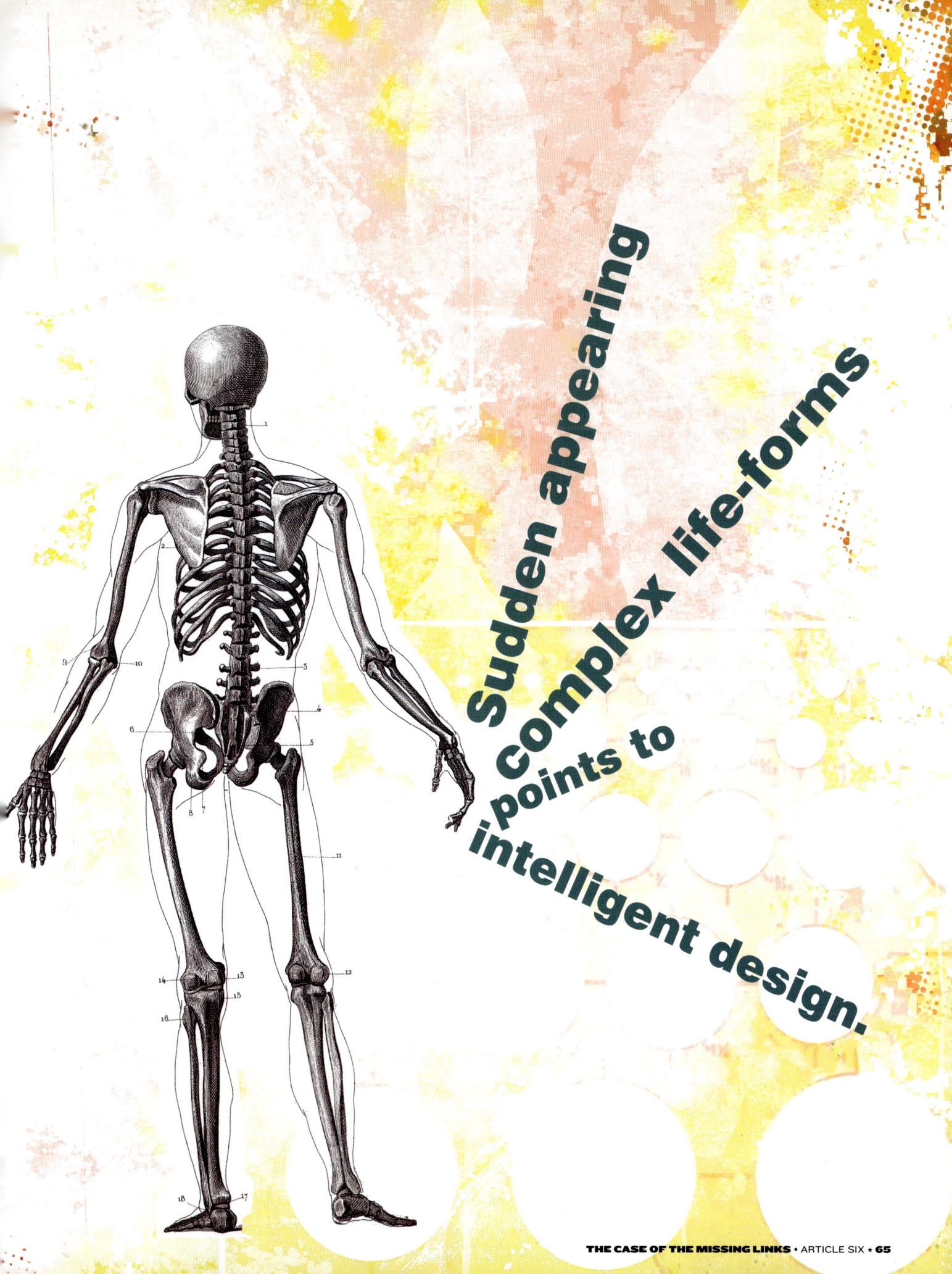

Sudden appearing complex life-forms points to intelligent design.

The discovery of DNA has revolutionized the world of forensic evidence. Cold case files have been reopened. Criminals who thought they had beaten the system have been belatedly prosecuted by a swab of saliva or body fluids forgotten about for decades. And in some instances, the new evidence has exonerated innocent prisoners.

Herman Atkins was just 20 years old when his life began to fall apart. He was imprisoned in January, 1986 for wounding three people in a shooting spree in South-Central Los Angeles. Prior to his imprisonment a "Wanted" poster had been widely circulated.

Later, at a sheriff's substation, a 23 year-old rape victim glanced at a "Wanted" poster on a nearby table that showed a young black fugitive from Los Angeles. In court, she testified that she turned to her mother and said, "That's him," and pointed at the picture of Herman Atkins.

A clerk from an adjoining business where the attacker stopped briefly before the rape also identified Atkins. Based primarily upon these eyewitness testimonies, the jury found Herman Atkins guilty of rape and robbery. His sentence: 47 years, 8 months in prison. Atkins spent thirteen years, three months, and six days in state prison, but not for a crime he had committed. His cold case had been reopened, and the DNA evidence had revealed that Atkins was not the rapist. On February 18, 2000 he walked out a free man, the victim of mistaken identity.

Just as DNA has revolutionized criminal forensics, the work of paleontologists has shed new light on human origins. Being an honest man, Charles Darwin made no bones (pardon the pun) about predicting that the forensic fossil evidence would ultimately prove his theory right or wrong.

But just as experts can jump to the wrong conclusion with regard to criminal evidence, so in the world of paleontology, a tooth, jaw, or piece of skull has often created premature headlines of "Missing Link Found." Paleontologist Michael Boulter summarizes the problem with identifying fossils correctly:

> It's very hard to piece together a few broken bones from a fossilized group of differentially aged primates scattered over a desert or cave floor and to be sure that they come from the same animal....It follows that the reliability of any description that attempts to recognize an actual species cannot be totally objective.[1]

Boulter is alluding to the fact that, being human, most scientists look at a fossil through the lens of their own presuppositions. For example, those who wanted to make a case for humans descending from apes were quick to jump with joy over the supposed discovery of the "missing link" called Piltdown Man. Featured in the *London Times*, *New York Times*, and various science journals, they made it a textbook example of the connection between apes and humans. However, forty years later, in 1953, it was revealed as a fraud.

Frauds like the Piltdown Man are rare, and although objectivity is often lacking, there is actually a wealth of fossil evidence depicting the history of life on our planet.

So in order to see what the forensic evidence says about Darwin's theory, we need to hear from paleontologists themselves about

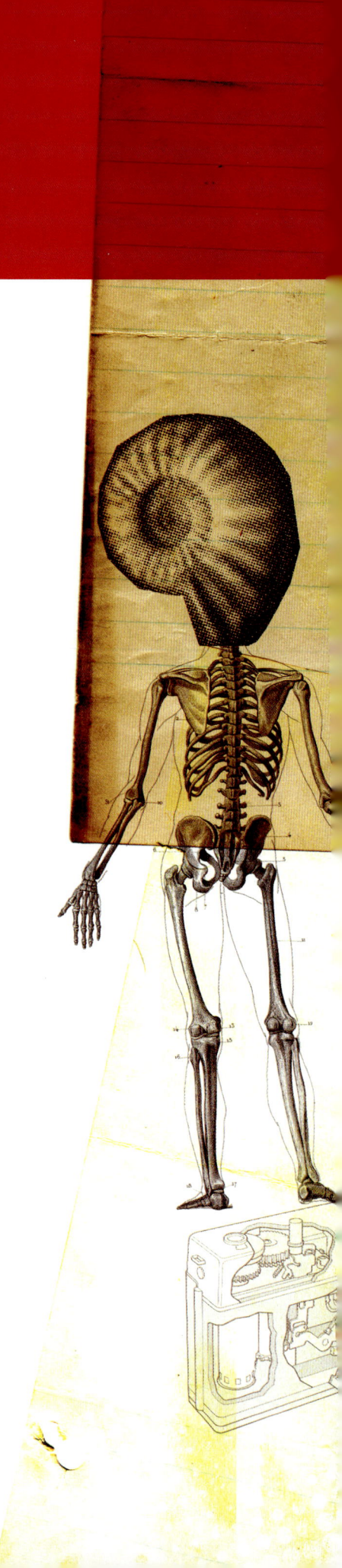

the evidence they have gathered during the nearly 150 years since he launched his theory. Our starting point is to clearly understand the predictions Darwin made regarding his theory and the fossils that should have resulted.

DARWIN'S TWO THEORIES

Charles Darwin was not the first to believe that life could arise by purely natural processes. In fact, the idea can be traced back as far as ancient Greece. And surely long before Darwin, people made the casual observation, "Hey, that guy kind of looks like a chimp." But it was Darwin who gave the ideas intellectual teeth, or viability, through his observation and hypothesizing of several processes, including adaptation and natural selection.

Few people realize that Darwin's theory of evolution predicts two different results: *microevolution* and *macroevolution*. We will look at microevolution first.

His micro-evolutionary theory states that variations within a species (cats, dogs, humans) can produce radical changes over time. He stated that sometimes these changes are accelerated by environmental conditions. For example, while on the Galapagos Islands, Darwin observed finches that had apparently grown slightly longer beaks during drought conditions. This confirmed his belief that creatures adapt to their environments.

Evolutionist Niles Eldredge explains the importance of adaptation to Darwin's theory: "Adaptation is the very heart and soul of evolution. It is the scientific account of why the living world comes in so many shapes and sizes: how the giraffe got its long neck, why porpoises look so much like sharks … how birds fly."[2]

Darwin believed that overpopulation of a species creates food shortages, which result in a struggle for survival, with the strongest of the species winning out. Kind of like *Survivor*, the winners pass on their genes to the next generation, improving the species, so life advances by survival of the fittest.

The evidence for Darwin's theory of change within a species is compelling. Bacteria do mutate and evolve. Cats, dogs, birds, and human beings all show evidence of variation predicted by Darwin. Some of us are tall, others short. Some thin, others…oops, better not go there.

The controversy surrounding Darwinian evolution is over his general theory of macroevolution. It states that over eons of time, all life evolved by the same process of natural selection. If true, then human beings are merely the end product of a long evolutionary chain. His belief in macroevolution is the reason Stephen Jay Gould was able to say that human beings are nothing more than "glorious evolutionary accidents."[3]

As we examine Darwin's general theory of macroevolution, we need to recognize that most biologists believe it provides the only scientific explanation for human origins. Materialists use this argument to reject intelligent design, saying it is "unscientific."

Biologists in general, have been far more reluctant to accept intelligent design as a valid option for the design evidenced in nature than their scientific counterparts in astronomy, physics, and cosmology. But that seems to be changing. In the face of stubborn opposition from the Darwinian paradigm, many biologists and paleontologists are now exposing Darwin's predictions to the scrutiny of scientific investigation, willing to follow the evidence wherever it leads. So let's see where it leads.

An increasing number of scientists are looking at the evidence from a common sense point of view. If macroevolution is right then it makes sense that the fossil record would prove Darwin right. So they begin by looking at the evidence that Darwin predicted would substantiate his claims. Darwin predicted that transitional fossil discoveries would eventually prove his theory right.

According to Darwin, these transitional fossils would provide ample evidence of gradual changes brought about by chance mutations.

The idea that one species could slowly change into another creates its own special problems, and because of these, Darwin championed the idea of favorable mutations. That is, the DNA of an organism would, on rare occasions, mutate favorably, which over time would lead to other favorable mutations, and the next thing you know, that ugly rat is now a cute little armadillo. Darwin assumed that life advanced over time from one-celled creatures all the way to humankind.

THE ROCKS TALK

We have observed examples of microevolution in which variations exist within a species. But there is little or no empirical evidence supporting Darwin's claim of macroevolution—one species evolving into another species.[4] More sophisticated creatures clearly do appear to arrive in later periods, but there remain yawning chasms (not mere gaps) between not only different species, but even between the highest orders of creatures, what are called phyla.

Why are the missing links essential to Darwin's theory? Couldn't gradual macroevolution have occurred without producing transitional fossils? Not according to Darwin. And certainly if countless species had undergone very gradual transitions from one category to another (for example, cats into dogs or fish into birds), then, according to Darwin, there should be countless fossils.

The abundance of transitional fossils should be demonstrable within all phyla and species, not merely a few. Certainly there should be many millions of transitional fossils, since it is estimated that over a billion species have existed in Earth's history. Again, we are not looking for microevolutionary changes of one type of bird evolving into another, or one type of horse evolving into another horse, etc.

Evolutionist Steven Stanley, a paleobiologist from Johns Hopkins, concludes in his book *Macroevolution* that, without the fossil evidence, "we might wonder whether the doctrine of evolution would qualify as anything more than an outrageous hypothesis."[5] In other words, all the conjecture about whether Darwinian evolution is factual or not comes down to hard evidence.

Occasionally some researcher claims to have "evolved" a new species in the lab, but that is not evidence for Darwinian macroevolution. In fact, many such claims turn out to be bogus, or merely evidence for microevolution. In any case, the lab experiment involves intelligence, not chance.

For 150 years paleontologists have been busy digging, classifying, and looking for these transitional fossils in a worldwide hunt. Billions of fossils representing about 250,000 species have been scrutinized. What have the scientists discovered? Does the fossil evidence support Darwin's theory of macroevolution? If it does, the missing links Darwin predicted should no longer be missing.

We commence our fossil search with the mysterious Cambrian period, an era geologists date at around 530 million years ago.

BOOM—LIFE

Seemingly out of the blue, complex life-forms with fully developed eyes appeared during the Cambrian period. It has been called by some "biology's big bang."

Only fossils for simple life-forms have been discovered from the time prior to the Cambrian period. Then, suddenly, the fossil record is shown to be teeming with more complex life-forms than exist today. It is called the "Cambrian Explosion."

Explosion is an apt term in this case. We see the period's importance, for example, in the appearance of new phyla. Phyla are the broadest category of animals that exist. According to biologists, you are a member of a phylum that also includes gerbils and trout. The differences between phyla are even more extreme than the differences within them. For example, the slug family falls into a separate phylum from that of humans. (So feel the freedom to squish them.) In fact, organisms in different phyla are built according to entirely different body plans.

What paleontologists find in the Cambrian explosion is not simply the appearance of a few new animals but the appearance of 50 completely different body types without prior transitions or predecessors.

Darwin staked his entire theory on the belief that a species could never suddenly appear.[7] He said, "If numerous species, belonging to the same ... families, have really started into life at once, that fact would be fatal to the theory of evolution through natural selection."[6]

Yet complex body organs such as eyes suddenly appeared during the Cambrian period. The trilobite eye has dozens of complex tubes, each with its own intricate lens. Darwinian gradualism cannot account for the sudden development of complex organs such as the fully formed eye.[7] Evolutionists are stumped because Darwin theorized that complex organs like the eye could only develop gradually over enormous periods of time, traceable to a common ancestor. Yet five totally different phyla with no hint of a common ancestor all suddenly popped into existence during the Cambrian period, each with fully developed eyes.[8]

T. S. Kemp, curator of the zoological collections at the Oxford University Museum of Natural History, is one of the world's foremost experts on Cambrian fossils. When discussing the sudden appearances of new species, Kemp declares, "With few exceptions, radically new kinds of organisms appear for the first time in the fossil record already fully evolved. ... It is not at all what might have been expected."[9]

Certainly new organisms with eyes developing quickly is not what Darwin had in mind when his theory defined natural selection as gradual changes over vast amounts of time. Oxford zoologist Richard Dawkins—no friend to a belief in creation—affirms, "Without gradualness ... we are back to a miracle."[10]

Stephen Gould, a staunch advocate of materialistic evolution, sums up the problem for Darwinists: "We do not know why the Cambrian explosion could establish all ma-

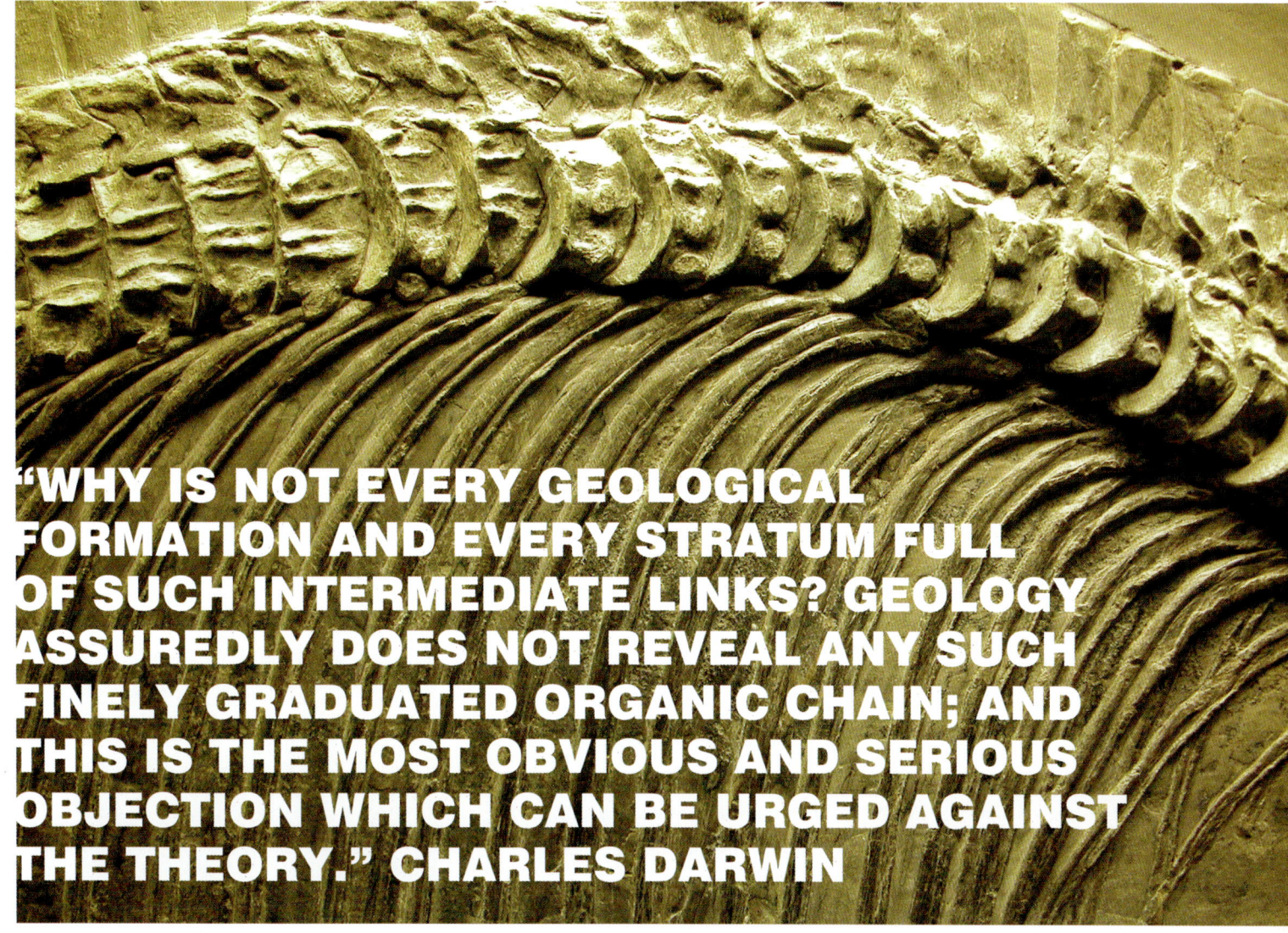

"WHY IS NOT EVERY GEOLOGICAL FORMATION AND EVERY STRATUM FULL OF SUCH INTERMEDIATE LINKS? GEOLOGY ASSUREDLY DOES NOT REVEAL ANY SUCH FINELY GRADUATED ORGANIC CHAIN; AND THIS IS THE MOST OBVIOUS AND SERIOUS OBJECTION WHICH CAN BE URGED AGAINST THE THEORY." CHARLES DARWIN

jor anatomical designs so quickly. ... The Cambrian explosion was the most remarkable and puzzling event in the history of life."[11]

Although the Cambrian explosion doesn't disprove Darwin's theory, it certainly does raise a huge question mark, and it has been a source of great frustration to materialists. But is the Cambrian explosion of suddenly appearing new species the only contradiction to Darwin's theory of macroevolution?

The best examples evolutionists offer in defense of macroevolution are the Archaeopteryx (a bird with reptilian features), and the Tiktaalik roseae (a fish that appears to have been developing limbs). But these two debatable examples don't explain the enormous gaps in the fossil record. Molecular biologist Michael Denton remarks, "Archaeopteryx was probably the best intermediate that Darwin was able to name, yet between reptiles and Archaeopteryx there was still a very obvious gap."[12] Darwin expected much more evidence to support macroevolution. This has led even the most ardent materialists to question Darwin's prediction.

Gould's colleague, Eldredge, frankly admits the failure of the fossil record to provide evidence for macroevolution, stating, "No one has found any such in-between creatures ... and there is a growing conviction among many scientists that these transitional forms never existed."[13]

LIFE-FORMS IN A RUT

What the fossil record does show, according to paleontologists, is that most species don't change but rather remain virtually the same for millions of years. They call this phenomenon *stasis*, which basically means you should not expect to grow a second head or third arm anytime in the foreseeable future.

Kemp forcefully summarizes the findings from the fossil record: "It is now indisputable that stasis ... occurs in ... probably a majority of cases of fossil species. ... Equally it seems beyond dispute that speciation [macroevolution] usually occurs so rapidly ... that the process is below the resolution of the fossil record."[14]

In other words evolution rarely occurs, and when it does, it occurs so rapidly it leaves no fossil trail. Eldredge remarks, "No wonder paleontologists shied away from evolution for so long. It never seems to happen."[15] But wait. Didn't Darwin theorize that all of life gradually evolved? How do Darwinists respond to this embarrassing lack of evidence?

According to Gould, with silence: "It's not evolution so you don't talk about it."[16] Gould, one of Darwin's strongest advocates, also admits, "The extreme rarity of transitional forms in the fossil record persists as the trade secret of paleontology. The evolutionary trees that adorn our textbooks have data only at the tips and notes of their branches; the rest is inference, however reasonable, not the evidence of fossils."[17]

Paleontologist Whitey Hagadorn has intensely studied fossils of the early marine animal communities, looking for evidence of transitions. He remarks, "Paleontologists have the best eyes in the world. If we can't find the fossils, sometimes you have to think that they just weren't there."[18]

> "IF NUMEROUS SPECIES, BELONGING TO THE SAME ... FAMILIES, HAVE REALLY STARTED INTO LIFE AT ONCE, THAT FACT WOULD BE FATAL TO THE THEORY OF EVOLUTION THROUGH NATURAL SELECTION."
>
> CHARLES DARWIN

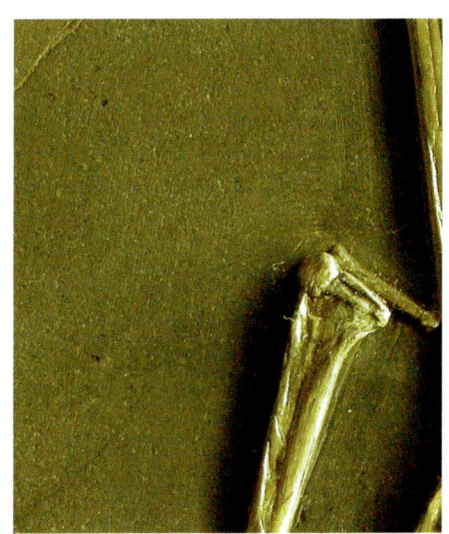

GRADUATING FROM GRADUALISM

Eldredge discloses that the Darwinian paradigm is so strong that paleontologists refused to admit defeat by acknowledging gradualism as wrong. "Paleontologists clung to the myth of gradual adaptive transformation even in the face of plain evidence to the contrary…"[19]

Eldredge and his colleague Gould, however, responded to the lack of transitional fossils by developing a new theory called *punctuated equilibria*, a complete departure from Darwin's basic premise of gradualism.[20]

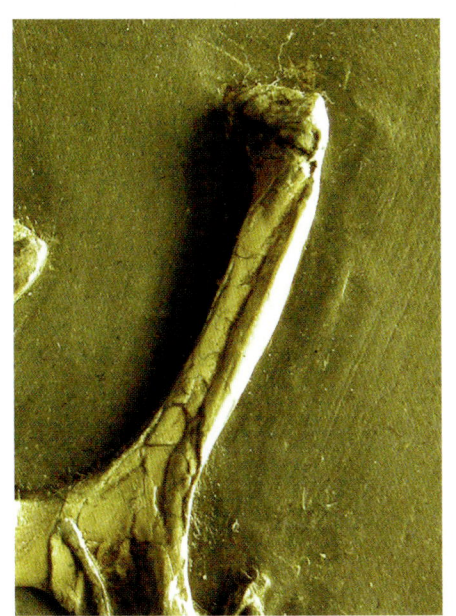

The punctuated equilibria theory contends that evolution, rather than being a gradual process, flourished quickly in small, isolated geographic regions, and then stabilized. But evolution was the exception, and rarely occurred.

Gould and Eldredge have argued that a sudden jump from species to species is the only way to explain the missing transitional fossils. Denton contests their conclusions are difficult to believe. "To suggest that … possibly even millions of transitional species … were all unsuccessful species occupying isolated areas and having very small population numbers is verging on the incredible."[21]

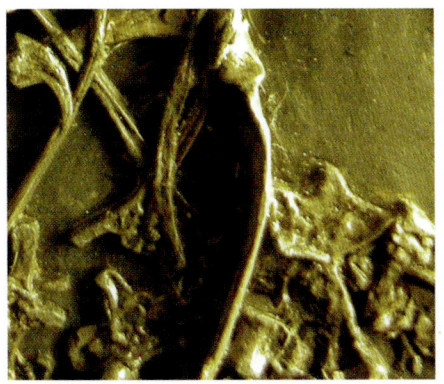

Whereas Darwin's theory required many millions of years, punctuated equilibria speculates that body forms evolved in hundreds of thousands of years, merely 100th of one percent of Earth's history. There is no known mechanism that can work so fast.

Based upon the fossil evidence, the following conclusions can be drawn:

1. Cambrian fossils contradict Darwin's theory.
2. Transitional fossils have failed to show up.
3. Most species don't change.
4. Perplexed materialists are seeking non-Darwinian explanations.

Gerald Schroeder cites how microevolutionary examples are used by Darwinists as "proof" of macroevolution: "…when the London Museum of natural History, a bastion of Darwinian dogma, mounted a massive exhibit on evolution, occupying an entire wing of the second floor, the only examples it could show were pink daisies evolving into blue daisies, little dogs evolving into big dogs, a few dozen species of cichlid fish evolving into hundreds of species of---you guessed it---cichlid fish. They could not come up with a single major morphological change clearly recorded in the fossil record. I am not anti-evolution. And I am not pro-creation. What I am is pro-look-at-the-data-and-see-what-they-teach."[22]

EVOLUTION WITH A PURPOSE?

Some scientists believe that the chemistry of life has been fine-tuned and that evolution was programmed into nature's laws. Conway Morris of Cambridge University, acknowledged as one of the foremost paleontologists of his time, has proposed a theory that combines design and evolution. Morris observes, "Far from being a random, directionless process, evolution shows deep patterns, and perhaps even a purpose."[23]

In his book *Life's Solution*, Morris makes a compelling case for inherent design in life.

Morris suggests that life could not have been a mere product of time plus chance, as Darwin theorized. He sees design and purpose in biological structures, pondering:

> Does evolution have a structure, an overall design, perhaps even a purpose? Orthodox opinion recoils from this prospect. Evolution, it is widely believed, is an effectively random process where almost any outcome is possible. … We, like all other life, are an evolutionary accident. But is this correct? In fact the evidence points in exactly the opposite direction.[24]

Morris cites evidence of design patterns like the eye, that exist in unrelated phyla. How did each of these unrelated animal groups develop an eye, independent of one another? Morris believes there are common patterns built into nature's laws. He calls his theory, *convergence*.

According to Morris, such common design patterns in totally separate phyla provide compelling evidence against Darwin's theory of accidental naturalistic evolution. But is designed evolution really an option if there is little or no fossil evidence to support macroevolution?

Although, like Morris, many believe in some form of directed evolution, such theories don't adequately explain the missing transitional fossils. Macroevolution, whether by design or by accident, still requires transitional forms. Yet the intense scrutiny of billions of fossils has failed to provide clear evidence for macroevolution other than a few debatable exceptions.

What, then, is the most plausible explanation for the missing transitional forms? There are really only three viable options:

1. *Darwin was right about macroevolution*. An abundance of transitional fossils will someday be found, or billions of transitionals were destroyed.
2. *Darwin was wrong about gradualism*. Macroevolution occurred rapidly, explaining the missing transitions (punctuated equilibria or design).
3. *Darwin was wrong about macroevolution*. The fossils can't be found because transitions never existed (design).

Paleontologists are not in agreement on which option is correct, but there is general agreement, with a few debatable exceptions, that the fossils that Darwin predicted would be discovered in abundance are truly missing. Materialists respond by showing fossil evidence of horses gradually evolving. But that is only microevolution. They also try to depict human evolution by assembling fragments of hominid skulls. But the origin of Homo sapiens has been a source of frustration and controversy. (See article 7)

As we have seen, Darwinist's best example, the Archaeopteryx, is a debatable transition between birds and reptiles. If Darwin was right, there should be millions of his

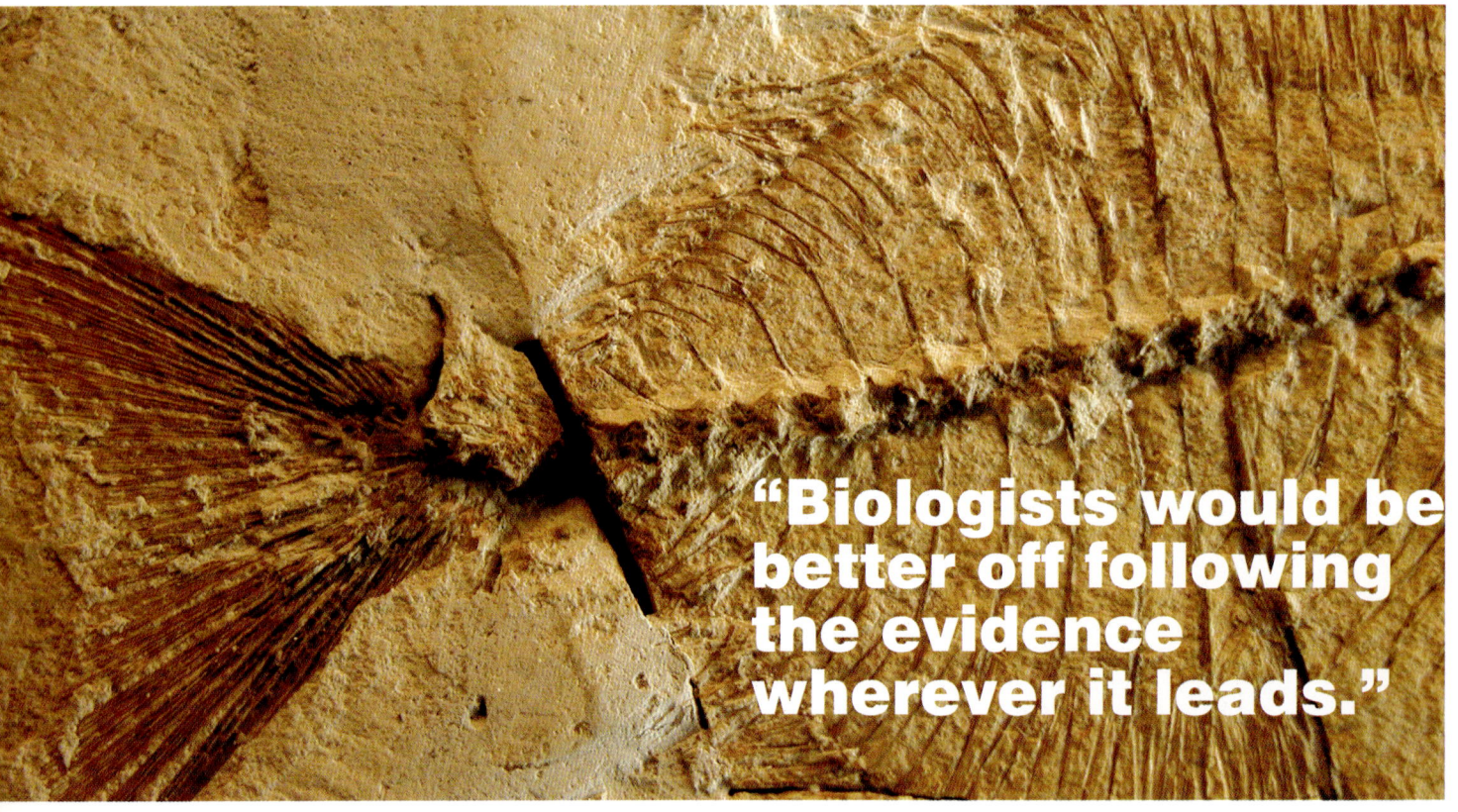

"Biologists would be better off following the evidence wherever it leads."

predicted transitional fossils forthcoming by now. That would end the debate.

DARWIN'S OWN VERDICT

In the case of Herman Atkins, DNA evidence proved that the original eyewitness testimony was flawed. Is it possible, that the combination of new evidence from molecular biology and the missing transitional fossils have revealed Darwinian evolution to be a flawed theory?

Biologists Mae-Wan Ho and Peter Saunders speak for many scientists who seriously question the claims of Darwin's theory:

> "It is now approximately half a century since the neo-Darwinian synthesis was formulated. A great deal of research has been carried on within the paradigm it defines. Yet the successes of the theory are limited to the minutia of evolution, such as the adaptive change in coloration of moths, while it has remarkably little to say on the questions which interest us most, such as how there came to be moths in the first place."[25]

"THE EXTREME RARITY OF TRANSITIONAL FORMS IN THE FOSSIL RECORD PERSISTS AS THE TRADE SECRET OF PALEONTOLOGY." STEPHEN JAY GOULD

Regardless of one's views of Charles Darwin, the geological record seems to have confirmed his worst fears; missing transitions, and the sudden appearance of new life forms. What Gould called the "trade secret" of paleontologists, the missing transitional fossils, points to the sudden appearance of new life forms, a phenomenon that Darwin said would be "fatal" to his theory of macroevolution.

Perhaps Gould's colleague Eldredge said it best when he admitted, "there is a growing conviction among many scientists that these transitional forms never existed."[26] And so we are left with a fossil trail that raises the question: How did these new life forms, some with fully developed eyes, appear so suddenly?

Many scientists reflect the view of Dr. Jonathan Wells, holder of PhDs in theology from Yale, and biology from Berkeley, who states, "Does this mean that biologists should devote their energies to proving the existence of a designer? I think not. It simply means that biologists should trust their common sense…biologists would be better off following the evidence wherever it leads."[27]

NOTES

1. Michael Boulter, *Extinction: Evolution and the End of Man* (London: Columbia University Press 2005).
2. Niles Eldredge, *Reinventing Darwin* (London: Phoenix Giant, 1995), 33.
3. Wim Kayzer, "*A Glorious Accident*" (New York: Freeman, 1997), 92.
4. Charles Darwin, *Origin of Species*, 6th ed. (New York: University Press, 1988), 413.
5. Steven Stanley, *Macroevolution* (San Francisco: Freeman, 1979), 2.
6. Darwin, 344.
7. Ibid.
8. Behe, 22.
9. T. S. Kemp, *Fossils and Evolution* (New York: Oxford University Press, 1999), 253.
10. Richard Dawkins, *River out of Eden* (New York: Basic, 1995), 83.
11. Stephen Jay Gould, "The Evolution of Life," *Scientific American*, October 1994.
12. Michael Denton, *Evolution: A Theory in Crisis* (Chevy Chase MD: Alder & Alder, 1986), 46-56.
13. George Alexander, "Alternative Theory of Evolution Considered," *Los Angeles Times*, November 19, 1978.
14. Kemp, 147.
15. Eldredge, 95.
16. Stephen Jay Gould, "Is a New and General Theory of Evolution Emerging?" (lecture, Hobart and William and Smith College, February 14, 1980).
17. Stephen Jay Gould, "Evolution's Erratic Pace," *Natural History*, vol. 86, May 1977, 14.
18. Quoted in, Thomas Hayden, "A Theory Evolves," *U.S. News & World Report*, July 29, 2002, 2.
19. Eldredge, 63.
20. Behe, 27–30.
21. Denton, 193–4.
22. Gerald L. Schroeder, *The Hidden Face of God* (New York: Touchstone, Simon & Schuster, 2001), 91.
23. Simon Conway Morris, *Life's Solution* (Cambridge: Cambridge University Press, 2003), front book jacket.
24. Darwin, 413.
25. M. H. Ho and P. T. Saunders, "Beyond Neo-Darwinism: An Epigenetic Approach to Evolution," *Journal of Theoretical Biology* 78 (1979), 589.
26. George Alexander, Ibid.
27. Quoted in William A. Dembski and James M. Kushiner, eds., *Signs of Intelligence* (Grand Rapids: Brazos, 2001), 127.

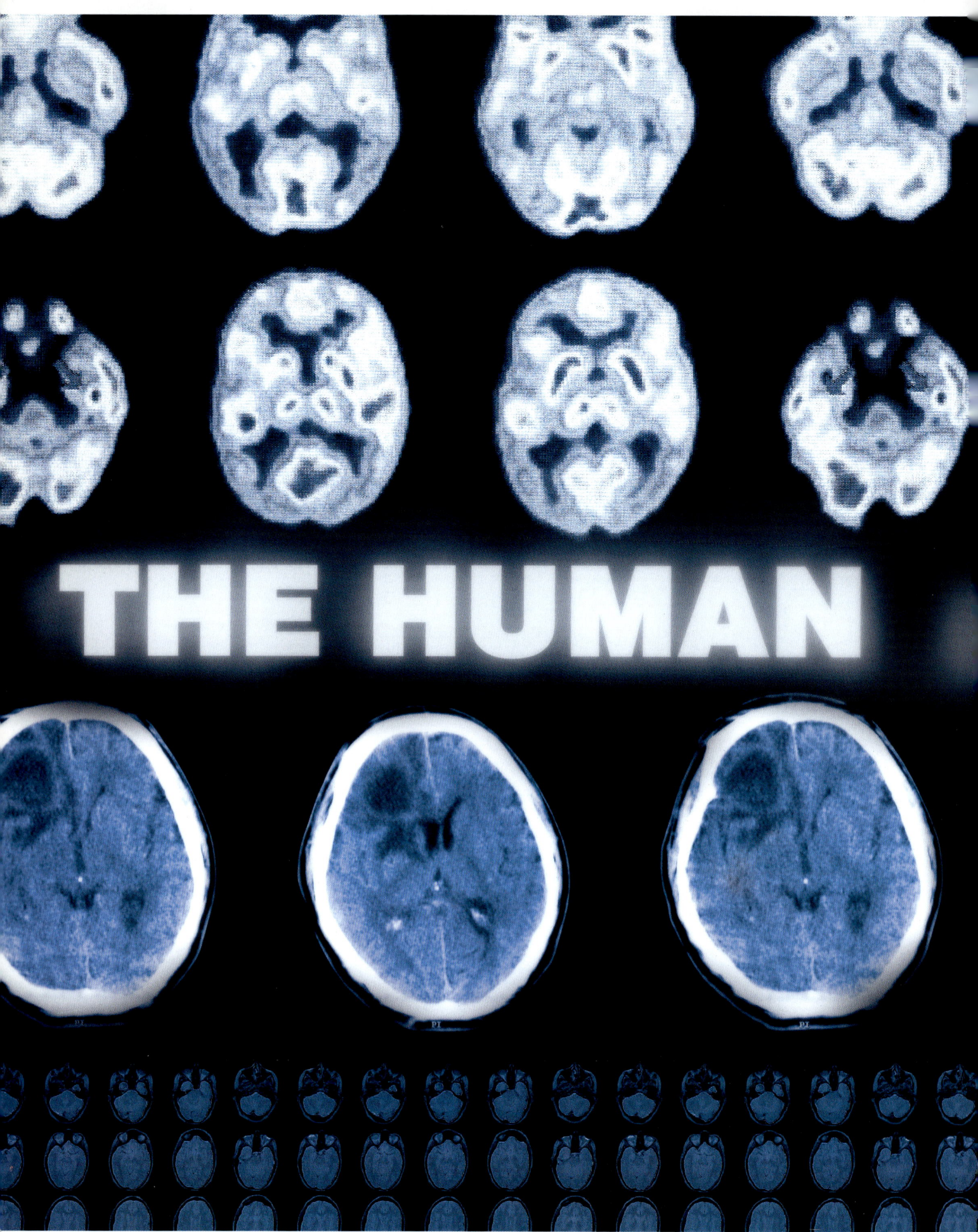

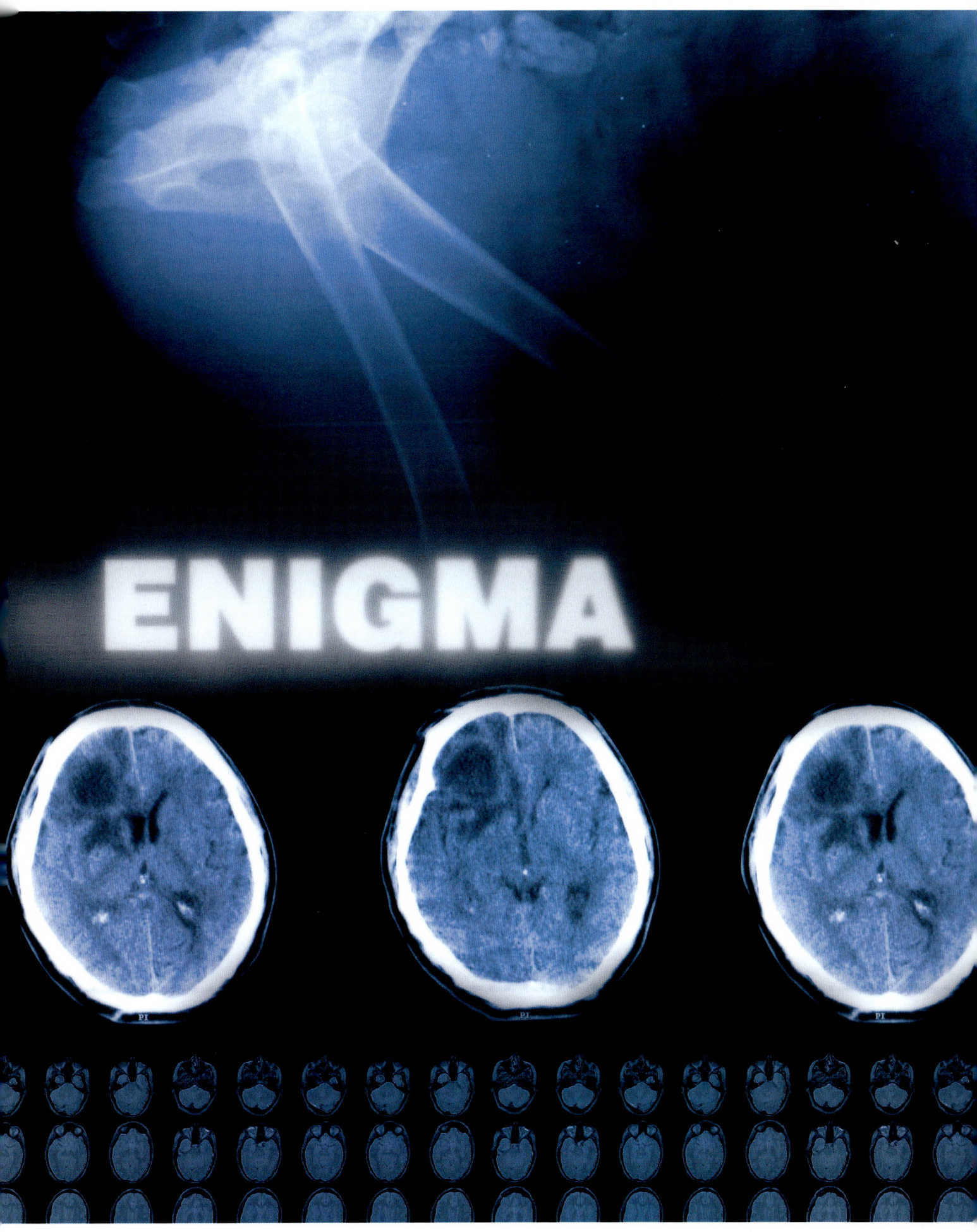

THE HUMAN ENIGMA • ARTICLE SEVEN

Scientific evidence indicates human beings are a unique species that is far superior to any species existing today or in the past.

In the movie, *Planet of the Apes*, Astronaut Leo Davidson is on a routine reconnaissance space mission in the year 2029, when suddenly his pod cruiser is thrust through a wormhole. Not knowing where they were, or how many years had advanced, he and his crew crash-land their cruiser on a strange planet that appears devoid of life. Suddenly they encounter an advanced tribe of intelligent talking apes who rule over a remnant of mute humans. Davidson's other crew members are killed by their brutal rulers, but he escapes to a desolate area called the Forbidden Zone, an area the apes greatly fear.

In the end, Davidson discovers that he has actually landed on Earth in the year 3978. And the Forbidden Zone is the desert-like remains from an ancient nuclear holocaust that wiped out humanity. A remnant of the Statue of Liberty is discovered in the dust, along with other reminders of a civilization that once was.

LOOK! A HUMAN BEING

It all looks and sounds so convincing. But what sounds like a solid argument for human ancestry unravels when the facts are made clear. Henry Gee, the chief science writer for *Nature* writes, "The intervals of time that separate fossils are so huge that we cannot say anything definite about their possible connection through ancestry and descent."[1]

The fossil trail has revealed creatures that seem to resemble apes, but have some human-like features. These members of the ape family that scientists call hominids are clearly not human, but evolutionists believe they eventually became us. Evolutionists begin with the premise that life is merely one large family tree (or bush).

They are looking for a trail of fossils that confirm Darwin's theory of macroevolution of our species. However, if evidence show that Homo sapiens appeared suddenly with qualities and traits distinct from all other forms of life, the possibility that we have been designed becomes apparent.

The problem is that paleoanthropologists are attempting to fill in an enormous puzzle with only a few fragments of bones and teeth that according to Gee, could be "fitted into a small box."[2] One of the most renowned evolutionists of the twentieth century, Stephen Jay Gould agrees with the difficulty, stating, "Most hominid fossils, even though they serve as a basis for endless speculation and elaborate storytelling, are fragments of jaws and scraps of skulls."[3]

Gould is not alone. Harvard zoologist Richard Lewontin also acknowledges: "when we consider the remote past, before the origin of the actual species Homo sapiens, we are faced with a fragmentary and disconnected fossil record." [4] Yet, these fragments of jaws and scraps of skulls, no matter how sparse and disconnected, have revealed some insightful clues about the uniqueness of our species. Let's dig deeper.

So have paleoanthropologists been able to bridge the chasm between what they call hominids and us, proving an evolutionary link?

We've all seen museum exhibits depicting slightly erect ape-like creatures that presumably became us. These exhibits and drawings in biology textbooks imply that there is solid fossil evidence to back up the claim that such fossils have been discovered. In fact, paleoanthropologists have uncovered pieces of bones and skull fragments from a variety of primates they consider human ancestors. Ardipithecus ramidus, the oldest of these, is dated at over 4 million years old. Homo habilis and Homo erectus are depicted as more recent members of our family tree.

The primary message is clear: human warfare and self-destruction enabled apes to evolve as the dominant species. But there is another, more subtle message: humans and apes are linked by an evolutionary family tree. Although the movie is humorous and entertaining, the message reflects the Darwinian paradigm that we are merely accidental beings in a chance world.

Actually, the entire Darwinian paradigm revolves around the theme that man is not unique, but rather just the end-product of a long evolutionary chain. The argument goes; that since we have bodies similar to apes, and since we share much of the same DNA, we must be related to them. Materialists cite this as proof that Darwin was right about us descending from lower forms of life.

It is not the purpose of this brief article to speculate on how life and the various species originated. A superintelligent designer could have created life in a number of different ways, either using natural laws, or transcending them. In fact, some scientists such as Simon Conway Morris, and Richard G. Colling, believe in designed evolution, where all of nature was intricately and ingeniously planned to eventually create you and me. The issue we address here is what leading scientists have discovered about our origins. In other words, what does the evidence reveal about our species––are we simply advanced apes, or are we unique and distinct? If the latter is true, it would certainly add credence to the argument that we have been designed.

THE HUMAN ENIGMA • ARTICLE SEVEN • 77

The first thing that strikes one as odd about Homo sapiens is their appearance on the stage of history. Despite the transitional drawings found in textbooks, intelligent, laptop-carrying man seems to have shown up rather abruptly.

Although small fragments of hominid bones have been discovered, there is a huge jump from such creatures to our own species. Naturalist Ian Tattersall (curator at the American Museum of Natural History) remarks in his book *The Fossil Trail*: "Something extraordinary, if totally fortuitous, happened with the birth of our species."[5] Tattersall is referring to the suddenness with which humans appear in the fossil record.

Biologists are unable to explain why our species appeared so suddenly. Professor John Maynard Smith, Emeritus of Biology at the University of Sussex writes, "Something very puzzling happened….The fossil evidence is patchy, but it seems that hominids suddenly developed brains that, in terms of size, were much like ours."[6] In other words, the jump from hominids to humans is unexplainable. No links have been discovered.

Most hominids had small, ape-like brains and no capacity for language. Then, suddenly in the fossil record, man appears with several unique features, including an enlarged brain capacity. Why are there no clear-cut links between hominids without language capacity and Homo sapiens?

SPEAKING OF SPEAKING…

The ability to speak distinguishes man from all apes and hominids. Although human beings have both the hardware and the software for language, hominids didn't. They didn't even come close.

According to noted evolutionist Ernst Mayr, humans have the ability to conceptualize, resulting in the development of art, literature, mathematics, and science. Hominids and all other animals lack this unique human quality, and are only able to communicate by giving and receiving signals.[7]

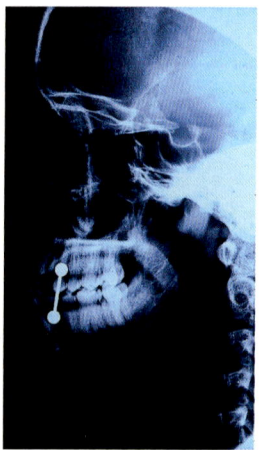

But even if man suddenly developed the ability to speak, what evolutionary advantage brought about the change? This presents a huge problem for those who argue against a designer.

As he traces the history of our species, evolutionist Steve Olson spells out the problem. "Of course, language could not have come from nowhere. To speak, early humans needed particular vocal and neural mechanisms. But here a notorious problem arises. Any adaptations produced by evolution are useful only in the present, not in some vaguely defined future."[8]

In other words, for human speech to work, the brain structure, the tongue, the larynx, the vocal cords, and many other parts all need to be fully developed.

Some biologists have speculated that a mutation occurred allowing an individual to talk. But, according to Olson, such explanations "have always been suspect." In reality, science cannot explain why we are the only creatures with the ability to speak.

UNIQUELY HUMAN?

Man's sudden appearance has scientists like Harvard scholar Lewontin pouring cold water on claims that a missing link between humans and apes has been discovered: Although he is an evolutionist, Lewontin acknowledges, "Despite the excited and optimistic claims that have been made by some paleontologists, no fossil hominid species can be established as our direct ancestor."[9]

The sudden appearance of man in the history of our planet has some scientists using the world "miracle." During an interview with the French science monthly *La Recherché*, Marcel Schutzenberger was asked, "The appearance of human beings—is that a miracle?"

The outspoken French mathematician replied,

> Naturally. And here it does seem that there are voices among contemporary biologists—I mean voices other than mine—who might cast doubt on the Darwinian paradigm that has dominated discussion for the past twenty years. Gradualists and saltationists [people

who believe in rapid species change] alike are completely incapable of giving a convincing explanation of the quasi-simultaneous emergence of a number of biological systems that distinguish human beings from the higher primates.

Schutzenberger was referring to several physiological differences between humans and primates for which no transitional fossils have been discovered.

He then concludes the interview with his view that there is no materialistic explanation for the sudden development of man: "The reality is that we are confronted with total conceptual bankruptcy."[10]

Even evolutionists like Mayr, who believe we descended from hominids writes: "Man is indeed as unique, as different from all other animals, as had been traditionally claimed by theologians and philosophers."[11]

Along the same lines, Ian Tattersall remarks on the uniqueness of humanity: "Homo sapiens are as distinctive an entity as exists on the face of the Earth, and should be dignified as such instead of being adulterated with every reasonably large-brained hominid fossil that happened to come along.[12]

Of all hominids, only Neanderthal had a large brain. Yet, Neanderthal was a distinct species according to DNA studies.[13] And, according to Olson they "seem not to have developed the fluent language that lets us wonder, adapt, and create."[14]

> "HOMO SAPIENS ARE AS DISTINCTIVE AN ENTITY AS EXISTS ON THE FACE OF THE EARTH, AND SHOULD BE DIGNIFIED AS SUCH INSTEAD OF BEING ADULTERATED WITH EVERY REASONABLY LARGE-BRAINED HOMINID FOSSIL THAT HAPPENED TO COME ALONG."
> IAN TATTERSALL

ONE HUMAN ANCESTOR?

So where did the human race originate, and does DNA confirm the uniqueness of our species? In *Mapping Human History*, Steve Olson traces the history of humankind through mitochondrial DNA analysis. By analyzing human fossils and DNA samples throughout history, new and stunning insights regarding human ancestry have been forthcoming:

1. *Once human beings appeared on the scene, there is no evidence of evolution.* Olson writes, "With the appearance of modern humans, the large-scale evolution of our species essentially ceased."[15]
2. *Human DNA is highly uniform compared with that of other species.* Olson remarks, "What must count as one of the most profound biological insights of all time is the recognition of our remarkable similarity."[16]
3. *Modern human beings originated and migrated from one area.* Paleoanthropologist at Cambridge University, Marta Lahr, explains, "The bulk of the chronological and genetic data indicate a single origin of all modern humans."[17]
4. *We have all descended from a single person.* Olson pens, "The first time I heard this statement I thought it highly implausible. All 6 billion people on this planet descended from a single ancestor? Yet this is one of those wonderful scientific conclusions that is not only true but *has* to be true."[18]

Thus mitochondrial DNA studies have shown that Homo sapiens not only arrived suddenly and recently on planet Earth, but have all orginated from a single ancestor.

What has caused mankind to transcend the animal world and probe space, develop computers, discover DNA, and create art and music? What makes us unique? The answer come down to three pounds of lumpy gray matter floating around in our heads.

THREE POUNDS OF LUMPY GRAY AMAZEMENT

So, what are we to make of the human brain? We generally associate complexity with intelligence. The more complex a building or machine, the more intelligence is required to engineer it. The human brain, for starters, contains 12 billion neuron cells intertwined with 100 trillion connections. To illustrate a number as large as 100 trillion, molecular biologist Michael Denton suggests visualizing a solid forest of trees covering half the United States. If each tree contains one hundred thousand leaves, the connections in a human brain would equal the total number of leaves in the entire forest.

Yet the brain's connections are not mere intersections like those in a highway system, but rather are a highly organized network far exceeding the complexity of all the communication networks on planet Earth.[19]

Our memories (one billion trillion bits of them) are not isolated in one section of the brain but instead are intertwined throughout the network. "Each junction has the potential to be part of a memory. So the memory capacity of a human brain is effectively infinite."[20] Inside that three pounds of gray matter of yours is enough information to fill 20 million books (19 million if you aren't that bright).

As we examine our universe, nothing else in it even remotely approaches the complexity of the human brain. Stephen Hawking compares the complexity of the human brain with most present-day computers and reveals the overwhelming superiority of our brains: "In comparison with most computers which have one central processing unit, the brain has millions of processing units ... all working at the same time."[21]

Even if communication engineers could apply the most sophisticated engineering techniques known to humanity, the assembly of an object remotely resembling the human brain would require an eternity of time. Even then, they still wouldn't know where to begin.[22] The overwhelming processing power takes place within an area of our brains called the cerebral cortex, and it is here where the human enigma is most apparent.

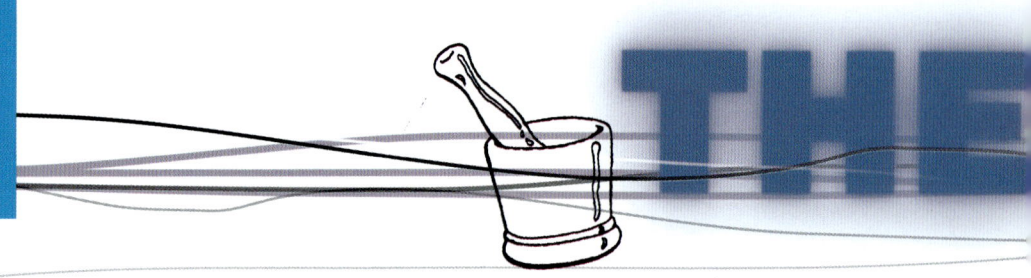

THE MYSTERY OF CONSCIOUSNESS

The cerebral cortex is the area of our brains where, mysteriously, "matter is transformed into consciousness."[23] The cerebral cortex distinguishes human beings from all other animals. "Though the difference between the human genome and that of a chimp is estimated to be less than 1 percent, our cerebral cortex has ten times more neurons."[24] But that is not the total story. Mayr reveals, "The unique character of our brain seems to lie in the existence of many (perhaps as many as forty) different types of neurons...."[25] And in spite of the DNA similarities, between humans and chimpanzees, there are still some 40 million differences.[26]

Additionally, recent studies have shown that chimpanzees lack awareness of their own thoughts, a trait that appears to be uniquely human. [27]

Awareness of thoughts is something that is beyond our ability to create, even in the most sophisticated software programs. When chess Grandmaster Gary Kasparov was defeated by the IBM supercomputer, Deep Blue, the computer didn't even realize it had won. Deep Blue lacked this self-awareness we take for granted. It is called consciousness, a mystery that has baffled philosophers and scientists for centuries.

Our awareness, with its manipulation of ideas, actually takes place in the prefrontal cortex.[28] It is here that we reason, ponder, imagine, fantasize, and seek answers to why we exisit. This prefrontal cortex area in a human makes up a far larger proportion of the cerebral cortex than in any animal, and it is the most complex arrangement of matter in the universe.[29]

If we could shrink in size and become spectators to the incredible activity in the innermost portion of the cerebral cortex, we might see something resembling a kaleidoscope of fireworks networking in all directions. Yet these electrical impulses are billions of organized patterns that result in our thoughts and imaginations. All of these thoughts intersect with our self-awareness.

While consciousness is at rest during sleep, the brain is still in action. "Even in sleep, the brain is pulsing, throbbing and flashing with the complex business of human life—dreaming, remembering, figuring things out. Our thoughts, visions and fantasies have a physical reality."[30]

Nobody really understands consciousness or how we got it. Sir John Maddox, former editor-in-chief of the journal *Nature*, addresses the puzzle of consciousness: "Nobody understands how decisions are made or how imagination is set free. What consciousness consists of, or how it should be defined, is equally puzzling. ... We seem as far from understanding cognitive processes as we were a century ago."[31]

For years materialists have tried to reduce humans to nothing more than a series of drives and instincts.

However, in reality human consciousness chooses between the instincts, and it is as different and separate from them as the pianist is from the keys he chooses to play on the piano. The consciousness sits over and above our instincts, drives, and desires, and it chooses which it will act upon.[32]

Thus, man can choose to disregard his own desire to survive for a higher purpose. Such an act of heroism works counter to Darwin's survival of the fittest, and is unexplainable by materialists. There seems to be something about consciousness that transcends self-preservation.

Another example of consciousness is the objectivity of the self—you distinguish yourself from your experiences. When stimulated, you distinctly feel that pain or pleasure is happening to you and that you are distinct from the experience causing the pain or pleasure. It is this objective awareness of our own thoughts that appears to be unique to human beings.

So difficult is the problem posed by our consciousness that Laurence C. Wood said, "Many brain scientists have been com-

pelled to postulate the existence of an immaterial mind, even though they might not embrace a belief in life after death."[33]

What process in natural selection could have led to human consciousness? Although evolutionists have taken a stab at it, no one really knows. Neither do scientists have an explanation for human imagination or creativity.

In human beings, the ability to simulate alternative future events appears to take place within our subjective consciousness. Oxford zoologist Richard Dawkins admits that nothing in Darwinian evolution accounts for it. Although Dawkins remains an ardent materialist, he writes, "Why this should have happened is to me, the most profound mystery facing modern biology."[34]

Even leading evolutionist Stephen J. Gould recognized the inability of natural selection to explain the human brain. Gould admitted, "I don't know why the brain got large in the first place. It certainly wasn't so that we could paint pictures or write symbols."[35]

DIFFERENT BY DESIGN?

Why did we get these incredibly complex brains with both the hardware and software for language? And according to evolutionists, our brains have remained unchanged. Mayr writes, "What is perhaps most astonishing is the fact that the human brain seems not to have changed one single bit since the first appearance of Homo sapiens...."[36] And where did consciousness and acts of heroism come from? There seems to be no evolutionary explanation for any of these unique human qualities.

In his book *What Evolution Is,* Ernst Mayr argues that our species is the only one of over a billion species that resulted in exceptional intelligence.[37]

So what are we to make of *us*? We create music and art. We dream and imagine. We endeavor to reach the stars, launching space shuttles and peering at the universe through powerful telescopes. And we wonder why we are here on this tiny speck called Earth. The enigma of man seems to point to something or someone beyond ourselves.

NOTES

1. Quoted in Lee Strobel, *The Case for a Creator* (Grand Rapids, MI: Zondervan, 2004), 62.
2. Ibid. 63.
3. Stephen Jay Gould, *The Panda's Thumb,* (W. W. Norton & Company, 1980), 126.
4. R. C. Lewontin, Human Diversity, (*Scientific American* Library, 1995), 163.
5. Ian Tattersall, *The Fossil Trail: How We Know What We Think We Know about Human Evolution* (Oxford: Oxford University Press, 1996), 246.
6. John Maynard Smith, "The Importance of Gossip," article in Rita Carter, *Mapping the Mind* (London: Phoenix Books, 2002), 257.
7. Ernst Mayr, *What Evolution Is* (New York: Basic Books, 2001), 253.
8. Steve Olson, *Mapping Human History: Genes, Race, and Our Common Origins* (New York: Houghton Mifflin Co., 2002), 87.
9. Lewontin, Ibid.
10. Marcel-Paul Schutzenberger, "The Miracles of Darwinism," *La Recherché*, January 1996.
11. Mayr, 252.
12. Tattersall, 219.
13. Fazale R. Rana, "Neanderthal-Human Link Severed, " *Connections*, Qtr 2, 2003, 8-9.
14. Olson, 29.
15. Ibid.
16. Ibid.
17. Ibid., 25.
18. Olson, 86.
19. Michael Denton, *Evolution: A Theory In Crisis* (Chevy Chase MD: Adler & Adler, 1986), 330-331.
20. Denton, 331.
21. Stephen Hawking, *The Universe in a Nutshell* (London: Bantam, 2001), 169.
22. Carl Sagan, *Cosmos* (New York: Ballantine, 1985), 229.
23. Gerald L. Schroeder, *The Hidden Face of God* (New York: Touchstone, 2001), 112.
24. Ibid.
25. Mayr, 252.
26. Nicholas Wade, "In Chimpanzee DNA, Signs of Y Chromosome's Evolution," *New York Times,* Sept. 1, 2005, A13.
27. C. D. L. Wynne, "The Soul of the Ape", *American Scientist,* 89 (2001), 120-122.
28. Carter, 312.
29. Ibid., 298.
30. Sagan, Ibid.
31. Sir John Maddox, "The Genesis Code by Numbers," *Scientific American*, December 1999, 62–67.
32. C. S. Lewis, *The Abolition of Man* (New York: Macmillan, 1947), 45–49.
33. Laurence W. Wood, *Asbury Theological Journal* 41, no.1 (1986).
34. Richard Dawkins, *The Selfish Gene* (Oxford: Oxford University Press, 1989), 59.
35. Stephen Jay Gould, quoted in Wim Kayzer, '*A Glorious Accident'* (New York: W. H. Freeman & Co., 1997), 93.
36. Mayr, Ibid.
37. Mayr, Ibid.

IMPRINTS OF DESIGN ON THE SOUL

While we can speak of the mind and the soul as distinct entities, we are often talking about the same thing. It is the opposite of what we mean by the brain, or the physical processes of intelligence. The nonmaterial aspect of who we are seems to defy reduction to physical processes. A case could be made that consciousness resides within the soul and that the soul itself is really the "I" or "ego" of what I am. But there is a slight distinction between mind and soul.

MIT-trained scientist Gerald Schroeder writes of this distinction. "Consciousness has all the trappings of another nonreducible element of our universe. The conscious mind is not mystical, but it may be metaphysical—meaning out of the physical."[38] In other words, consciousness is not explainable in natural terms and has the transcendent characteristics of a totally different dimension. Perhaps this is why materialists are so baffled by the enigma of consciousness.

While our "mind" seems to refer to all of the mechanisms of consciousness, the "soul" seems to speak of a spiritual or religious impulse that resides within humanity. This spiritual instinct, perhaps the clearest of all indicators of intelligent design, can be seen in some of the following phenomena.

Innately religious. Since the dawn of recorded time, and in every place on the globe, people have been religious. Belief in God, some say, is something that people are taught to believe, but both archeology and sociology would tell us otherwise. People are innately religious, with over 90% of the world's population believing in some divine power. Wherever you go, people instinctively bow to the heavens. It would seem that religious belief is not something people are reasoned into but something they are persuaded out of.

Oughtness. Have you ever seen a cow that seems disillusioned with life and who thinks she was made for something better? (OK, besides the Chick-fil-A cows.) Unlike cows in the pasture, most humans have a sense that things are not as they should be. A longing for heaven, it has been called. We struggle with circumstances, resent death, complain of evil, and have a general sense that we were made for something better, that things "ought" to be different. Why do we have these thoughts? Why shouldn't we simply accept life on its own terms?

Morality. When someone commits a terrible crime, doesn't something inside us scream for justice? Think of the Holocaust or September 11th when terrorists flew airplanes into the World Trade Center buildings, killing nearly 3,000 innocent people. We all share a common sense of horrible injustice and desire for retribution.

Materialists believe morals come from society, but are unable to explain a moral reformer such as Martin Luther King who applied Christian principles to promote black Americans' civil rights.

Materialists also struggle to explain how the German culture could justify the genocide of 6 million Jews during the Holocaust of World War 2. Hitler convinced many Germans that eliminating the Jews was a worthy act since he deemed them an inferior race. The butchery, torture, and medical experimentation during this period originated from a culture that for the most part justified such behavior. Yet we intuitively know it was wrong. But why? This inner moral sense of right and wrong cannot be attributed merely to society or culture, but seems to point to something beyond ourselves.

If the elements of consciousness, spirituality, oughtness, and morality are not primarily physical, then materialism will never be able to account for them. But what are they? Could they be imprints from a transcendent designer who has programmed us with an image of his own DNA?

IMAGINE THE DESIGNER

THE UNIVERSE NOT ONLY IMPLIES THE EXISTENCE OF A DESIGNER BUT SUGGESTS SOMETHING ABOUT WHAT HE MIGHT BE LIKE

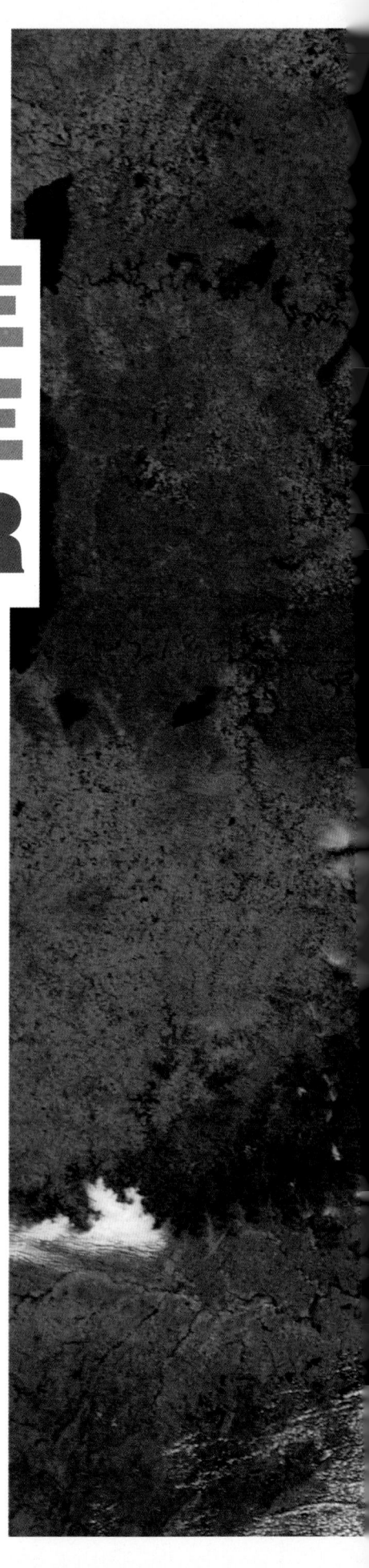

In the movie *Contact*, Jodi Foster portrays Ellie Arroway, a beautiful young scientist obsessed with finding intelligent life on other planets. One day, as Ellie monitors radio transmissions from space, a coded message flashes across her computer screen. The stunned Ellie realizes that intelligent beings have communicated with Earth from beyond our galaxy.

Decoding the instructions, Ellie and her colleagues discover the encrypted blueprint for an advanced spacecraft that will transport them to the distant galaxy, millions of light years from Earth. Once the spacecraft has been built, Ellie is chosen to become its sole passenger.

Although Ellie's boyfriend objects, her passion for meaning in life overpowers her love for him. Turning to him, Ellie explains her reason for leaving him: "I've been searching for something, some reason why we are here. What are we doing here? Who are we?"

Ellie speaks for many of us who wonder about life. Who are we, and why are we here? (Actually, some of you may be wondering about more mundane things, like what's for dinner, or what *she* thinks of you.)

Has science, with its new discoveries in outer space and inside the molecular world, reached a point where it can shed light on such profound questions? Never has there been a more exciting time in the history of science. What does the fine-tuning of cosmos and intricate complexity of DNA mean to us?

WHAT OR WHO IS BEHIND ALL THIS BRILLIANCE?

HAS A DESIGNER LEFT ANY CLUES ABOUT HIS NATURE OR HIS PURPOSE?

THESE ARE THE QUESTIONS SCIENTISTS, AS WELL AS THE REST OF US WHO ARE INTERESTED IN THE RESULTS OF THEIR EXPLORATION, ARE DRAWN TO ASK.

ADMITTING THE APPEARANCE OF DESIGN

In light of recent discoveries, many leading scientists have had their materialistic presuppositions challenged. One of those, Sir Fred Hoyle, was a world-renowned astronomer and founder of the Institute of Astronomy at Cambridge.

Although Hoyle remained an agnostic, the brilliant astronomer remarked, "A common sense interpretation of the facts suggests that a superintellect has monkeyed with physics, as well as chemistry and biology."[1]

Hoyle is not alone. Other great scientists have alluded to the compelling evidence for design in the universe, yet have been unwilling to ask the question of who planned it, or to delve into the reason behind the universe. Stephen Hawking admits scientists' reticence to probe questions of our origins, stating, "There must be religious overtones. But I think most scientists prefer to shy away from the religious side of it."[2]

However, there are scientists who are not so shy, and are asking profound questions: Why is the universe so finely-tuned for life? Has a designer left his fingerprints? Why are we here?

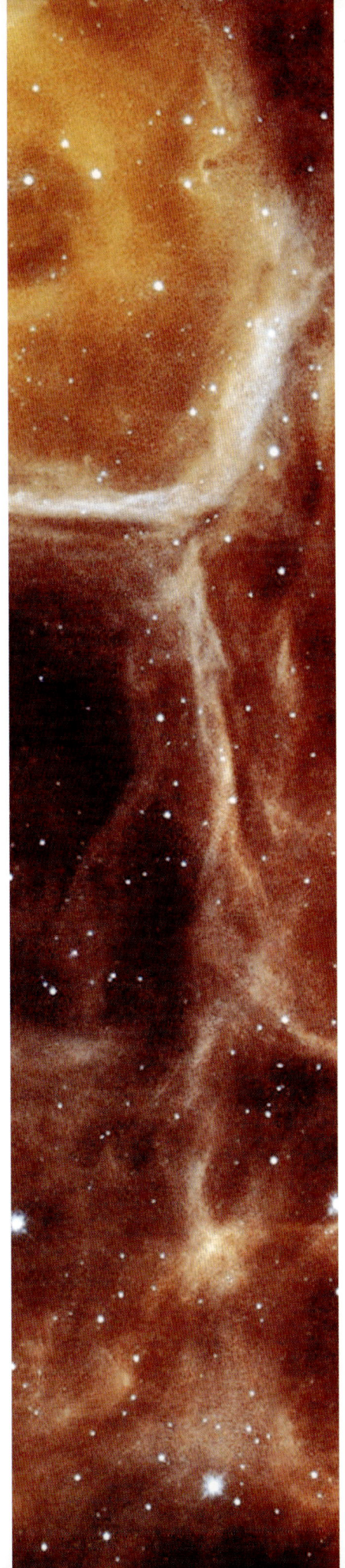

> "THERE MUST BE RELIGIOUS OVERTONES. BUT I THINK MOST SCIENTISTS PREFER TO SHY AWAY FROM THE RELIGIOUS SIDE OF IT."
>
> STEPHEN HAWKING

ASKING DEEPER QUESTIONS

Although Hawking tries to avoid religious discussion, he still asks,

> What is it that breathes fire into the equations and makes a universe for them to describe? The usual approach of science of constructing a mathematical model cannot answer the questions of why there should be a universe for the model to describe.
>
> Up to now, most scientists have been too occupied with the development of new theories that describe *what* the universe is to ask the question *why*. On the other hand, the people whose business it is to ask *why*, the philosophers, have not been able to keep up with the advance of scientific theories.[3]

Here Hawking opens up new territory for scientists. Since Copernicus, and especially after Darwin, materialism had ruled the day in science. Any reference to God was scoffed at as a "God of the Gaps" argument, another way of saying "God is merely a stop-gap explanation for lack of knowledge, and has no place in our materialistic universe." But now it is scientists who are actually initiating the discussion about an intelligent designer.

Theoretical astrophysicist George Greenstein, in his book, Symbiotic Universe, asks, "Is it possible that suddenly, without intending to, we have stumbled upon the scientific proof of the existence of a Supreme Being? Was it God who stepped in and so providentially crafted the cosmos for our benefit?[4]

Greenstein is a luminary in his field, being a professor of astronomy at Amherst College and a recipient of the Phi Beta Kappa Award in Science. This isn't Forrest Gump here, scratching his head at the complexity of it all or attributing to God what he simply can't grasp. Neither are other scientists who, like Greenstein, are looking at the scientific evidence and pondering the reality of God.

WHAT KIND OF DESIGNER?

If leading scientists like Greenstein are right in their conclusions that a designer exists, are there things that can be deduced about his nature from the observation of the universe? Why did he create us? Has he left any clues about our purpose here on planet Earth? Although these questions move beyond science into the realm of natural theology, they have been provoked by new discoveries in science.

So, if a designer has left clues about himself, where would we look for them? To begin our search, we need to examine the universe to see if he has left his fingerprints. Just as the paintings of The Last Supper and Mona Lisa tell us something about their artist, Leonardo Da Vinci, and Beethoven's Fifth Symphony reveals clues about its composer, we should be able to discern clues about a designer by observing his universe.

Although scientific evidence only gives us a partial picture of what a designer is like, the universe does reveal some insightful clues about his nature.

The following characteristics seem to emerge. The designer is a
- purposeful designer
- powerful designer
- superintelligent designer
- personal designer

Once scientists discovered the remarkable fine-tuning of the universe, many reasoned there must be a purpose behind it. Paul Davies, one of the leading theoretical physicists in the world, writes, "If the universe has been designed by God, then it must have a purpose."[5]

Mathematician Roger Penrose –who, with Hawking, derived proof for the beginning of time –offers his insight:

> There is a certain sense in which I would say the universe has a purpose. It's not there just somehow by chance. Some people take the view that the universe is simply there and it runs along –it's a bit as though it just sort of computes, and we happen by accident to find ourselves in this thing. I don't think that's a very fruitful or helpful way of looking at the universe. I think that there is something much deeper about it, about its existence, which we have very little inkling of at the moment.[6]

Penrose deduces that the fine-tuning of physical constants (see article 3) for man's existence is so improbable that it must have been intentionally planned. And it follows that whoever intentionally created the universe has a purpose that must include us. In his book, Superforce, Davies writes,

> The laws which enable the universe to come into being spontaneously seem themselves to be the product of exceedingly ingenious design. If physics is the product of design, the universe must have a purpose, and the evidence of modern physics suggests strongly to me that the purpose included us.[7]

If purpose is apparent from the fine-tuning of the universe, its awesome power is evident from startling new discoveries made possible by Hubble and other high-powered telescopes. Consider a few of the latest findings:

- Black holes have such powerful gravitational force that even light cannot escape their grasp. Large ones gobble up stars like our Sun as mere snacks. (Maybe yummy…but a little too hot).[8]
- Supernova eruptions are so powerful that their light can rival the visual brightness of an entire galaxy with 100 billion suns. The resulting neutron star is so dense that on Earth, one teaspoonful would weigh a billion tons![9]
- Quasars generate the energy of 100 galaxies, shine with the intensity of a trillion suns, and reach temperatures of several million degrees.[10]
- Gamma-ray bursts have the power of 10 billion billion suns. A single gamma-ray burst is capable of obliterating life on Earth in milliseconds.[11]

Power demonstrated by great earthquakes and thermonuclear explosions would be virtually insignificant when contrasted with that of black holes, gamma-rays, or quasars. Yet, even those are miniscule when compared with the power demonstrated at the beginning of the universe. Scientists are not only amazed at the power within the cosmos, but even more in awe of the power required to create and control it all.

> "IS IT POSSIBLE THAT SUDDENLY, WITHOUT INTENDING TO, WE HAVE STUMBLED UPON THE SCIENTIFIC PROOF OF THE EXISTENCE OF A SUPREME BEING? WAS IT GOD WHO STEPPED IN AND SO PROVIDENTIALLY CRAFTED THE COSMOS FOR OUR BENEFIT?"
>
> GEORGE GREENSTEIN, SYMBIOTIC UNIVERSE

Scientists are also in awe at the incredible genius behind the universe. Arguably the greatest mind in the history of science, Albert Einstein acknowledges that the mind behind the universe is a "superintelligence of such superiority that, compared with it, all the systematic thinking and acting of human beings is an utterly insignificant reflection." [12] Einstein acknowledged this intelligence without ever defining it in personal terms.

Perhaps with DNA engineering, man will discover ways to increase human intelligence or develop supercomputers far more advanced than Deep Blue, the IBM version that defeated Grandmaster Gary Kasparov in chess. But as Einstein notes, we can't compare human genius with the intelligence of the one who designed it along with the universe and its laws of physics, quantum mechanics, and the intricate complexity of DNA? Astronomer Hugh Ross explains that it is impossible to impose any limit on either the power or intelligence of a transcendent Creator.[13] That is because the Creator would not be restricted by any of the constraints of our four-dimensional world–including time.

Think for a minute of a being outside of time and the limitations of gravity and other natural forces. Our natural laws would have no power over him since he would be in complete control of them. And, being outside of time, he would know everything in the past–present–and future.

But is the Creator of the universe merely an energy force like a microwave or is he personal like us? Is he aloof and non-relational like *The Force* in *Star Wars*? If so, how was an impersonal force capable of creating personal, relational beings? This is the question that has puzzled both scientists and philosophers.

In *Contact*, Ellie Arroway supposedly discovers the purpose she had been yearning for, but not from a personal creator. After returning from her encounter with an advanced civilization, Ellie tells her Christian friend Palmer,

The story I have to tell you isn't exactly about Punishment and Reward…. There's not a word in it about Jesus. Part of my message is that we're not central to the purpose of the Cosmos.[14]

Ellie continues, "The universe was made on purpose….In whatever galaxy you happen to find yourself, you take the circumference of a circle, divide it by its diameter, measure closely enough, and uncover a miracle–another circle, drawn kilometers downstream of the decimal point. There would be richer messages farther in. It doesn't matter what you look like, or what you're made of, or where you come from. As long as you live in this universe, and have a modest talent for mathematics, sooner or later you'll find it." Sagan ends his novel with this message: "She found what she had been searching for." [15]

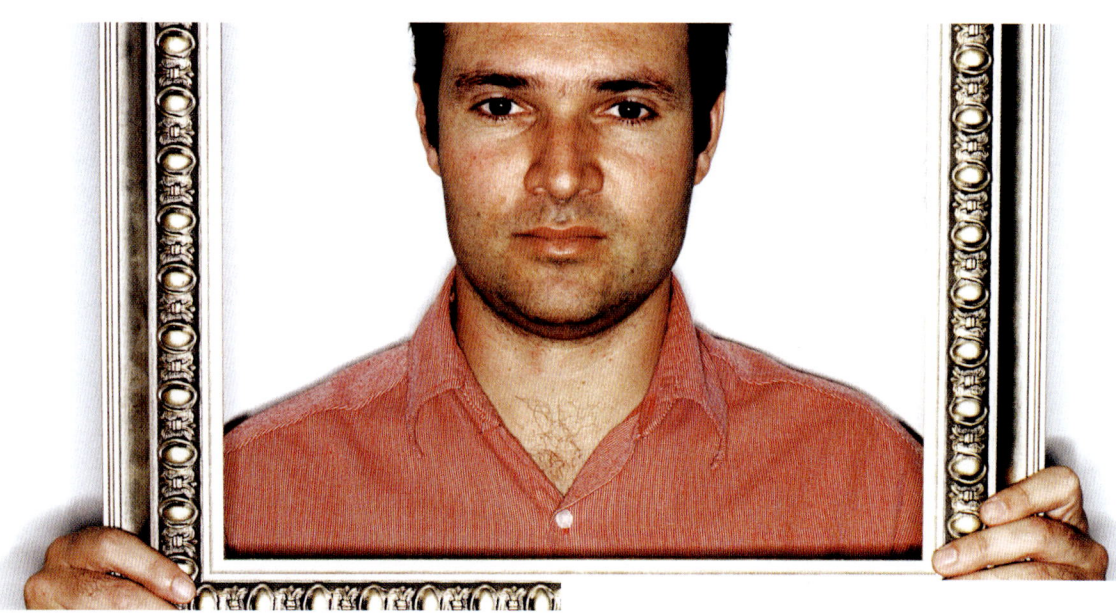

HAS THE DESIGNER SPOKEN?

Is it possible that an impersonal, mathematical force like Ellie's circles is behind everything in the cosmos? In his book, *The Kalam Cosmological Argument,* Dr. William Lane Craig argues that it isn't. He states that a beginning to the universe proves that its Creator is personal. Craig summarizes the possibilities:

1. The universe either (a) had a beginning or (b) had no beginning.
2. If it had a beginning, the beginning was either (a) caused or (b) uncaused.
3. If it had a cause, the cause was either (a) personal or (b) not personal.[16]

Therefore, since the evidence clearly points to a universe that had a primary cause, it logically follows that the cause was personal. According to Craig, intelligence, volition (will), and power are all implied in the act of creating. If we think about a painting such as the Mona Lisa, we see the same things. Leonardo Da Vinci needed intelligence, volition, and power to paint the image he wanted to portray. These attributes point to Da Vinci being a person, and not a mere force.

Philosopher Francis Schaeffer concurs, asserting, "No one has ever demonstrated how…an impersonal being can produce the needed complexity of the universe, let alone the personality of man."[17]

> NO ONE HAS EVER DEMONSTRATED HOW AN IMPERSONAL BEING CAN PRODUCE THE NEEDED COMPLEXITY OF THE UNIVERSE, LET ALONE THE PERSONALITY OF MAN
>
> FRANCIS SCHAEFFER

Yet, in spite of these arguments for a personal creator, materialists remain unconvinced. They speak of a cold, uncaring universe that has originated by undirected forces blindly operating through eons of time. They believe in a universe without any purpose. But some startling new evidence recently brought forth seems to challenge their skepticism.

In *The Privileged Planet*, theologian Jay Richards and astronomer Guillermo Gonzalez reveal a startling fact: Earth has been placed in an optimal location for scientific observation of our universe.[18]

In other words, if Earth was in a slightly different position in our solar system or galaxy, or located in another galaxy, we might find ourselves looking at a night sky with no stars to observe. Or the sky might be so flooded with light that we couldn't distinguish one star from another. If we didn't have this optimal position, many of the discoveries about our universe would have been impossible.

Imagine being in a large room with many seats and one tiny window with a view of space. One front row seat has a view, while the occupants of other seats can't see out. Earth's position in the universe is like having that front-row seat. Our front-row seat to the universe isn't part of the fine-tuning requirement for life, but it seems to have been given to us intentionally. Richards and Gonzalez conclude that a designer wants us to know and understand his universe.

At this point many might ask, "so what? How does that impact my life?" The obvious next question is, has a personal creator related to us in ways we can better understand? And if so, where do we look to discover more about his nature, and what he has said about our purpose?

Agnostic George Smoot has remarked that an obvious parallel exists between the big bang and the Christian teaching of creation from nothing.[19] Smoot takes his inference to the Christian God no further, presumably leaving it for theologians.

Theology, like philosophy or science, makes logical deductions –in this case, logical deductions about the nature of God. So let's see what we can logically deduce from what science has told us about God. Since we have seen evidence from science and logic that the Creator of the universe is purposeful, powerful, superintelligent, and personal, he certainly would understand our desire to know more about him and his purpose for creating us.

A creator who intentionally designed us with consciousness, personality, and the ability to communicate would be able to communicate with us if he so desired. Just as SETI is searching outer space for messages from intelligent beings in other galaxies, so we would expect a personal creator to have given us a message in a way we could understand. Of all creatures on Earth, humans are the only ones who are able to communicate propositional ideas –and we do it through written and spoken language.

Although our brief attempt to make sense of the universe cannot possibly look at each religion or its god, Smoot's assertion that a parallel exists between the scientific evidence for a beginning and the Christian teaching of creation deserves a deeper look.

The Judeo-Christian Bible remarkably presents a God who is purposeful, powerful, superintelligent, and personal. It speaks of this God as an infinite, eternal Creator, who alone made everything there is from nothing. Although he is presented as a fearsome God of law and order, he is also shown to be a God of love who created us for a relationship with himself.

Well, perhaps we should stop here. But we can't resist taking our logic one more step. If God were really there, and if he revealed himself through science, and even through the written word, would that be sufficient? Would that show the highest order of care and communication? We're persuaded that it would not.

If you really love someone, sending them an email every month or so just wouldn't cut it. Sooner or later, if you really care, you'll be compelled to drop in for a visit –show up and get involved in his or her life.

We close by suggesting that God may in fact have done just that –"shown up." Here we leave physics and chemistry and biology, and turn to history, a field of human inquiry that can also provide knowledge about the real world.

As we examine the history of mankind, is there any evidence that a designer has paid us a visit –and actually dropped in on us? Is it possible that God has visited Earth in human form? Many laugh at such an idea, recalling numerous ancient myths and legends that utter tales of superhuman gods visiting Earth. However, if the Creator paid us a visit, we would not be looking for a myth, but a real person who has transformed history.

Whereas history records the feats of many great people, only one person has truly transformed history. Yale historian, Jaroslav Pelikan tells us his name: "Jesus of Nazareth has been the dominant figure in the history of Western culture for almost twenty centuries." When the great secular historian, H. G. Wells was asked what person had the biggest impact upon world history, he answered, "By this test, Jesus stands first."

But historical impact is only one element of Jesus' uniqueness. There are several other reasons why this one man is worthy of a deeper look. His life, his reported miracles, and his claims, convinced his followers that he was more than a mere man. They left a written record that Jesus was the one who put the stars in space, established the laws of the universe, and created you and me.

But were they deluded? Or could the entire account of Jesus have been a conspiracy like The *Da Vinci Code* asserts? Was Jesus Christ just a great man who was later deified by the Roman emperor, Constantine and the fourth century church? Or are the written accounts in the New Testament right? Did the Creator actually drop in on us and pay us a visit?

These all-important questions about this intriguing person are the subject of another investigation: *Y-Jesus*. In the *Y-Jesus* magazine which is about the most fascinating person in history, we examine evidence outside the Bible and tradition in order to solve the mystery of Jesus' true identity. And if he is really who he claimed to be, we want to know what he said about you and me, and our purpose in the universe.

As we contemplate our place on this remote planet in a universe of ten billion trillion stars, we come back to the question, are we accidents, or are we special?[18]

Materialist Stephen Jay Gould considered us lucky to be alive—"the glorious accident resulting from 60 trillion contingent events." Yet, as leading scientists examine the universe, another picture is beginning to emerge. Many of these scientists are convinced that we are a divine conception, the intentional work of a powerful, superintelligent, purposeful designer. If true, we are special.

> As we examine the history of mankind, is there any evidence that a designer has paid us a visit—and actually dropped in on us?

NOTES

1. Fred Hoyle, "Let There Be Light," *Engineering and Science* (November 1981).
2. Quoted in John Boslough, *Stephen Hawking's Universe* (New York: Avon, 1989), 109.
3. Stephen Hawking, *A Brief History of Time*, 174.
4. George Greenstein, *The Symbiotic Universe* (New York: William Morrow, 1988), 27.
5. Paul Davies, *God and the New Physics* (New York: Simon & Schuster, Touchstone, 1984), 199.
6. Stephen Hawking, ed., *Stephen Hawking's A Brief History of Time: A Reader's Companion* (New York: Bantam, 1992), 142.
7. Paul Davies, *Superforce* (New York: Simon & Schuster, 1984), 243.
8. William Keel, "Quasars Explained," *Astronomy*, vol. 31, no. 2 (February, 2003), 42-47.
9. Ibid. Alexei Fileppenko, "When Stars Explode," 42-47.
10. Keel, 35-41.
11. Jan van Paradijs, "From Gamma-Ray bursts to Supernovae," *Science*, 286 (1999) 693-95.
12. Albert Einstein, *Ideas and Opinions—The World As I See It* (New York: Bonanza, 1931), 40.
13. Hugh Ross, *Beyond the Cosmos* (Colorado Springs, CO: NavPress, 1996), 100–102.
14. Carl Sagan, *Contact* (New York: Simon & Schuster, Pocket Books, 1985), 420.
15. Ibid., 430, 431.
16. William Lane Craig, *The Kalam Cosmological Argument* (Eugene, OR: Wipf & Stock, 2000), 63.
17. Francis A. Schaeffer, *He Is There and He Is Not Silent* (Wheaton, IL: Tyndale House, 1976), 9.
18. Guillermo Gonzalez and Jay W. Richards, *The Privileged Planet* (Washington, D.C.: Regnery, 2004).
19. George Smoot & Keay Davidson, *Wrinkles in Time* (New York: Avon Books, 1993), 17.

QUOTES

FRED HOYLE (BRITISH ASTROPHYSICIST)
"A common sense interpretation of the facts suggests that a superintellect has monkeyed with physics, as well as with chemistry and biology, and that there are no blind forces worth speaking about in nature. The numbers one calculates from the facts seem to me so overwhelming as to put this conclusion almost beyond question."

GEORGE ELLIS (BRITISH ASTROPHYSICIST)
"Amazing fine tuning occurs in the laws that make this [complexity] possible. Realization of the complexity of what is accomplished makes it very difficult not to use the word 'miraculous' without taking a stand as to the ontological status of the word."

PAUL DAVIES (BRITISH ASTROPHYSICIST)
"There is for me powerful evidence that there is something going on behind it all. It seems as though somebody has fine-tuned nature's numbers to make the Universe. The impression of design is overwhelming."

ALAN SANDAGE (WINNER OF THE CRAWFORD PRIZE IN ASTRONOMY)
"I find it quite improbable that such order came out of chaos. There has to be some organizing principle. God to me is a mystery but is the explanation for the miracle of existence, why there is something instead of nothing."

JOHN O'KEEFE (NASA ASTRONOMER)
"We are, by astronomical standards, a pampered, cosseted, cherished group of creatures. If the universe had not been made with the most exacting precision we could never have come into existence. It is my view that these circumstances indicate the universe was created for man to live in."

GEORGE GREENSTEIN (ASTRONOMER)
"As we survey all the evidence, the thought insistently arises that some supernatural agency—or, rather, Agency—must be involved. Is it possible that suddenly, without intending to, we have stumbled upon scientific proof of the existence of a Supreme Being? Was it God who stepped in and so providentially crafted the cosmos for our benefit?"

ARTHUR EDDINGTON (ASTROPHYSICIST)
"The idea of a universal mind or Logos would be, I think, a fairly plausible inference from the present state of scientific theory."

ARNO PENZIAS (NOBEL PRIZE IN PHYSICS)
"Astronomy leads us to a unique event, a universe which was created out of nothing, one with the very delicate balance needed to provide exactly the conditions required to permit life, and one which has an underlying (one might say 'supernatural') plan."

ROGER PENROSE (MATHEMATICIAN AND AUTHOR)
"I would say the universe has a purpose. It's not there just somehow by chance."

TONY ROTHMAN (PHYSICIST)

"When confronted with the order and beauty of the universe and the strange coincidences of nature, it's very tempting to take the leap of faith from science into religion. I am sure many physicists want to. I only wish they would admit it."

VERA KISTIAKOWSKY (MIT PHYSICIST)

"The exquisite order displayed by our scientific understanding of the physical world calls for the divine."

STEPHEN HAWKING (BRITISH ASTROPHYSICIST)

"What is it that breathes fire into the equations and makes a universe for them to describe? …

Up to now, most scientists have been too occupied with the development of new theories that describe *what* the universe is to ask the question *why*?"

ALEXANDER POLYAKOV (SOVIET MATHEMATICIAN)

"We know that nature is described by the best of all possible mathematics because God created it."

ED HARRISON (COSMOLOGIST)

"Here is the cosmological proof of the existence of God—the design argument of Paley—updated and refurbished. The fine tuning of the universe provides prima facie evidence of deistic design. Take your choice: blind chance that requires multitudes of universes or design that requires only one. Many scientists, when they admit their views, incline toward the teleological or design argument."

EDWARD MILNE (BRITISH COSMOLOGIST)

"As to the cause of the Universe, in context of expansion, that is left for the reader to insert, but our picture is incomplete without Him [God]."

BARRY PARKER (COSMOLOGIST)

"Who created these laws? There is no question but that a God will always be needed."

DRS. ZEHAVI, AND DEKEL (COSMOLOGISTS)

"This type of universe, however, seems to require a degree of fine tuning of the initial conditions that is in apparent conflict with 'common wisdom'."

ARTHUR L. SCHAWLOW (PROFESSOR OF PHYSICS AT STANFORD UNIVERSITY, 1981 NOBEL PRIZE IN PHYSICS)

"It seems to me that when confronted with the marvels of life and the universe, one must ask why and not just how. The only possible answers are religious. . . . I find a need for God in the universe and in my own life."

HENRY "FRITZ" SCHAEFER (COMPUTATIONAL QUANTUM CHEMIST)

"The significance and joy in my science comes in those occasional moments of discovering something new and saying to myself, 'So that's how God did it.' My goal is to understand a little corner of God's plan."

WERNHER VON BRAUN (PIONEER ROCKET ENGINEER)

"I find it as difficult to understand a scientist who does not acknowledge the presence of a superior rationality behind the existence of the universe as it is to comprehend a theologian who would deny the advances of science."

QUESTIONS ABOUT ORIGINS

Q. WHAT NEW DISCOVERY IN ASTRONOMY HAS PROVOKED MANY LEADING SCIENTISTS TO RETHINK THE ORIGIN OF OUR UNIVERSE?

A. Most scientists thought the universe had always existed until Edwin Hubble observed that the universe is expanding. Scientists now believe that the universe originated with a one-time explosion of incredible force called, "the big bang." But scientists wonder how everything in our cosmos could come from nothing. Something or someone must have been there to cause it to begin. Astrophysicist George Smoot (an agnostic) said, *"If you're religious, it's like looking at God."*
(See article 1)

Q. HOW COULD A "BIG BANG" RANDOMLY RESULT IN THE CONDITIONS NECESSARY FOR LIFE?

A. Scientists have calculated that several conditions vital for life needed to be fine-tuned to a razor's edge. Without this precise fine-tuning, our universe wouldn't exist, let alone support life.

Leading astrophysicist Stephen Hawking writes, *"The odds against a universe like ours emerging out of something like a big bang are enormous.... I think there are religious implications whenever you start to discuss the origins of the universe."* (See article 2)

Q. HOW DO SCIENTISTS ACCOUNT FOR SUCH INCREDIBLE ODDS AGAINST LIFE EXISTING ON EARTH?

A. Many scientists admit that a finely-tuned universe, and a "just right" solar system and planet couldn't have happened without a superintelligence. Others chalk it up to an incredible coincidence.

A few prefer to believe a speculative theory, that there may an astronomical number of universes, and that ours just happens to be the one that supports life. However, theoretical physicist, Paul Davies confides what many scientists conclude, *"It seems as though somebody has fine-tuned nature's numbers to make the Universe....The impression of design is overwhelming."*
(See article 3)

Q. COULD INTRICATE ORGANS LIKE THE EYE HAVE EVOLVED BY UNGUIDED NATURAL PROCESSES?

A. Darwinian natural selection doesn't explain how the eye's many individual components could independently evolve, yet synchronize together to produce sight. Several molecular biologists conclude that irreducibly complex systems, like the eye, have been designed. Even Darwin admitted that the eye still gave him a "cold shudder." (See article 4)

Q. CAN DNA'S DETAILED CODING BE EXPLAINED BY NATURAL PROCESSES?

A. DNA's intricate complexity caused its co-discoverer, Francis Crick, to call it "almost a miracle." Since no scientific process, including natural selection, is able to explain DNA's origin, many scientists believe that it must have been designed. Antony Flew was so impressed by the genius behind DNA that he renounced 50 years of atheistic leadership, arguing that DNA must have been designed by a superior intelligence. (See article 5)

Q. DOES EVIDENCE SUPPORT DARWIN'S THEORY THAT ALL LIFE EVOLVED BY UNDIRECTED NATURAL PROCESSES?

A. Evidence supports Darwin's theory of *microevolution*, where environmental adaptations result in variations within a single population, such as a species. This is why viruses mutate, house insects have evolved resistance to our pesticides, and dogs, cats, and humans, come in various shapes sizes and colors. Scientists are correct when they state Darwinian microevolution is factual.

However, Darwin's theory of *macroevolution*, says that over time, undirected natural processes led to all life forms, from the most primitive cell to human beings. He predicted countless fossils would prove him right. But the transitional fossils Darwin predicted would validate macroevolution are embarrassingly absent. Even ardent evolutionist, Niles Eldredge admits, *"No one has found any such in-between creatures...and there is a growing conviction among many scientists that these transitional forms never existed."* (See article 6)

Q. WHAT DO DNA AND THE FOSSIL TRAIL REVEAL ABOUT HUMAN ORIGINS?

A. Mitochondrial DNA studies have shown that our species originated from one location, and one mother (they call Eve). Although fossil hunters have discovered a few extinct species of hominids, these creatures are vastly inferior to humans in their intellectual capacities. Thus paleoanthropologists remain baffled by the single origin and sudden appearance of Homo sapiens in the fossil trail. (See article 7)

Q. IF A DESIGNER EXISTS, HAS HE GIVEN US CLUES THAT REVEAL WHAT HE IS LIKE?

A. Many scientists believe that a designer has put his "fingerprints" on the cosmos. Theoretical physicist Paul Davies writes, *"If physics is the product of design, the universe must have a purpose, and the evidence of modern physics suggests strongly to me, that the purpose included us."* The evidence seems to indicate that the designer is not just purposeful, but that he is also personal, superintelligent, and immensely powerful. (See article 8)

Q. WHY DO SCIENTISTS DISAGREE ABOUT THE EVIDENCE FOR DESIGN?

A. Some scientists, regardless of the evidence, cannot accept intelligent design because they are adamantly opposed to the possibility that God is involved in the development of life. Others deny the existence of any higher power. Like Stephen Jay Gould, they believe that we are merely "cosmic accidents."

On the other hand, an increasing number of scientists have recognized evidence for intelligent design behind all the laws of science and the fine-tuning in the universe. Intelligent design proponents advocate *"following the evidence, wherever it leads."*

Q. ARE INTELLIGENT DESIGN AND BIBLICAL CREATIONISM THE SAME?

A. Although some mistakenly lump them together, their premise is so different it's like comparing apples and oranges. Biblical creationism looks at science through the lens of Genesis, whereas intelligent design draws its inferences about our origins from scientific discoveries without any such filter. Intelligent design advocates vary in their religious beliefs, and leave the identity of the designer to theologians. Biblical creationists, on the other hand, specify the designer as the Judeo-Christian God. An increasing number of scientists believe that the discoveries in science point more and more to a position totally consistent with the Bible.

ABOVE QUESTIONS FOR FACILITATING INDIVIDUAL OR GROUP STUDY

RECOMMENDED BOOKS

The following books are recommended as additional resources on both the origin of the universe and the origin of life. Although different viewpoints are expressed in these materials, they are recommended for a reader's better understanding of the subjects.

THE PRIVILEGED PLANET, GUILLERMO GONZALEZ & JAY RICHARDS

A unique perspective on cosmology which systematically builds the argument that planet Earth is not merely designed for human life, but also human discovery of the cosmos. For the serious science reader.

BEYOND EINSTEIN: THE COSMIC QUEST FOR THE THEORY OF THE UNIVERSE MICHIO KAKU & JENNIFER THOMPSON

A compelling read on the history of string theory in theoretical physicists' quest to solve the riddle of how two radically different principles, quantum physics and relativity, can both operate within the cosmos.

THE ELEGANT UNIVERSE, BRIAN GREENE

Greene attempts to take the very difficult science of string theory and make it interesting. This material has become the subject of a PBS television special by the same name.

WRINKLES IN TIME, GEORGE SMOOT & KEAY DAVIDSON

This well written book provides a chronology of how scientists discovered the birth of the universe and confirmed its beginning with the COBE Satellite's remarkable discovery. Smoot recalls his personal experiences as head of the project.